Manna-Free Living

- Why do I need to understand the difference between debt-free and manna-free?

- Why do I need to know the difference between Source and Resource?

- Why did the manna cease, and why am I still looking for it?

- Why is Struggle Class more than an issue of money?

- Why does God have me on my current payment plan?

- Why is it important that my life be thoroughly furnished before my lifestyle?

Manna-Free Living

- Why do I need to understand the difference between debt-free and manna-free?

- Why do I need to know the difference between Source and Resource?

- Why did the manna cease, and why am I still looking for it?

- Why is Struggle Class more than an issue of money?

- Why does God have me on my current payment plan?

- Why is it important that my life be thoroughly furnished before my lifestyle?

R. CARNELL JONES

Pleasant Word
A Division of WINEPRESS PUBLISHING

Pleasant Word (a division of WinePress Publishing, PO Box 428, Enumclaw, WA 98022) functions only as book publisher. As such, the ultimate design, content, editorial accuracy, and views expressed or implied in this work are those of the author.

Unless otherwise noted, all Scriptures are taken from the Holy Bible, New International Version, Copyright © 1973, 1978, 1984 by the International Bible Society. Used by permission of Zondervan Publishing House. The "NIV" and "New International Version" trademarks are registered in the United States Patent and Trademark Office by International Bible Society.

Scripture references marked NKJV are taken from the New King James Version of the Bible.

Scripture references marked KJV are taken from the King James Version of the Bible.

Scripture references marked AMP are taken from the Amplified Version of the Bible.

ISBN 1-4141-0437-5
Library of Congress Catalog Card Number: 2005902502

Dedication

Dedicated to my loving and supportive wife DeLaine, my wonderful children Christian, Alicia, and Grant, and my New Hope Fellowship family. Thank you for encouragement, patience, and prayers.

Table of Contents

Foreword

Manna was the main food supply of the Israelites for forty years. It's, therefore, no great surprise that Numbers 11:6 records them losing their appetite for it. It wasn't until they entered into Canaan, however, that God's abundant provision became available to them. Likewise, many of us have wearied of the ongoing limitations of our resources; yet something deep within tells us that God has so much more for us. To access God's bounty we have to cross the border into the Promised Land and end our dependency on manna.

This Bible study consists of an in-depth analysis of over seventy-five Scripture references on the subject of the resources God has provided you. Each of the nine units has:

- "Life speaks" scenarios that set a 21st century stage for the biblical information in the unit
- Multi-formatted, thought-provoking review questions
- a "Unit Jewel" highlighting a major unit point
- a "Unit Summary" recapping the unit focus
- a Meditation/Prayer Focus

The goal of this Bible study is to assist Christians who desire help in the areas of:

- Developing a closer relationship with God through their resources
- Bringing stability to their resources
- Becoming better stewards of their resources
- Maximizing and multiplying the power of their resources

I pray that you are blessed by this work and will join me in daring to believe that God wants miraculous provision to flow through us and not just to us.

Introduction

Debt-Free or Manna-Free?

The thought of being debt-free is wonderful. But we can be debt-free, yet not God-honoring with our finances. Although many debt-free resources encourage tithes and offerings, their primary focus remains teaching the "how to" of getting out of debt; this is needed. *Manna-Free Living,* however, focuses more on the "why to" of honoring God with the finances that He has entrusted to us. As we gain a better understanding of the "why" from a biblical perspective, we are more likely to implement the "how" in a manner that benefits the kingdom of God as well as ourselves.

For Christians who realize the vital connection between their finances and God's agenda, being manna-free is a mandatory precursor to being debt-free. While debt-free and manna-free can be complementary concepts, the fact is that most people have some amount of debt. And in our drive to either manage or alleviate debt, kingdom needs are often put on hold. We must reverse this spiritually unhealthy trend and become Christians who, regardless of whether we have debt or not, remain God-honoring.

> Then the manna ceased on the day after they had eaten the produce of the land; and the children of Israel no longer had manna, but they ate the food of the land of Canaan that year.
>
> —Joshua 5:12 (NKJV)

Miraculously and generously it fell from the sky; yet manna was only food for the Israelites as they traveled through the wilderness. Manna was a sign that a loving God would always meet the needs of His people, but it could not match the inheritance that awaited the children of Israel in the Promised Land of Canaan. Today, God's miracles and provision continue, but the manna has ceased. It is, therefore, time to put our personal wilderness experiences behind us. Instead of continually looking heavenward for God's blessings to rain down upon us, we must start going forward with God's Spirit accompanying us. In terms of our resources, we must biblically assess where we are and why we are there. This will equip us with the knowledge to journey to the Promised Land and enjoy the blessings of manna-free living.

Source and Resource

Life Speaks: Darren and Nicole Carter

Darren and Nicole are Christians who attend church maybe once a month. They would like to become more active in their church, but their business, Marketing Solutions, takes all of their time. By most standards their business would be considered successful. But even though they have ample income, they don't feel they are currently able to support the church financially.

It's been three years since the inception of their business and they feel it's only a matter of time before it becomes a huge success, at which point they will begin to get more involved in the work of the church. Darren and Nicole have made the all-too-common mistake of allowing the resource of money to become the source and focus of their lives.

Confusing the Source and the Resource

God is the eternal Source providing for our needs by using the resource of money. Problems arise when we make the resource our source. While we may say that God is the hub that our whole world revolves around, we must be careful that our actions don't reveal that money is at the center of our affection.

God is a perfect Source because He has an inexhaustible supply of everything we need. The problem with making money our source is that it's always running out, and we have to work too hard to maintain it. Therefore to view money as a source is a set up for disappointment. Money was never meant to be "the" Source. It was always meant to be a "re"source.

Is there any "Re" in your resource?

The prefix "re" means "again." So the true meaning of "resource" is "to spring up again", or "to arise anew." We need to find ways to make our money do this. If it's not springing up again, then it's not a true resource.

Think about it. We get paid, buy groceries, pay bills, purchase a few other things, and the money is gone. It doesn't spring up again in our account. It springs out! We may call it a resource, but really there is no "re" in our resource. Money is not our Source, and because of how we can misuse it, it isn't always a reliable resource.

We need to determine if our resources have any "re" in them. The "re's" that we don't want to hear are those informing us that something has been revoked or rejected and needs to be reexamined or reviewed; or if something isn't done, something is going to get reported, or may have to be reconnected or repossessed. When we're confused on source and resource, we can get the wrong set of "re's" attached to our sources.

We need a source that is constant and maintains itself; a source that is full of "re." God is that Source. He can restore, redeem, refine, refresh, relieve, renew, repair, and reward. Our God is full of "re"! Natural resources become depleted, so we need a supernatural Source to bring the necessary natural resources into our lives.

Going into the T.O.M.B.

We all know how to earn money, but we must learn how to make our money grow. A starting point is learning how to go into the T.O.M.B. T is for tithing. O is for giving offerings. M is for maintaining our household necessities. B is for paying bills on time. If those four things take all of our money, then so be it! Going into the T.O.M.B. means death to old spending habits. This death will eventually lead to a glorious resurrection of our financial resources.

It's called a tomb because it's a very dark and dreadful place to our flesh. We give tithes and offerings to reaffirm God's position as our Source. We buy the basics for our households, and we pay bills. That doesn't sound like a whole lot of fun, but we have to ask ourselves, "Do I want to eat manna forever, or do I want to stay in the T.O.M.B. for a season in order to get to the Promised Land?" Success or failure hinges on the answer to this question.

Once we become disciplined in the T.O.M.B., four more letters come into play. D.E.S.I.D is for debt reduction. We should graduate from merely paying bills on time to aggressively paying them off. E is for enjoyment. At this point we deserve a break. We can occasionally treat ourselves to something nice without undoing all the progress we have made so far. S is for savings. Start a savings plan. No amount is too small as a starting point. I is for investments. Whether it is stocks, a dream, or the kingdom, begin investing! When we become disciplined in doing these things, we will have gained a good understanding of source and resources.

T.O.M.B.D.E.S.I.

Until we understand source and resource, we will unwisely remove letters from the T.O.M.B.D.E.S.I. acronym. We will have a hard time bringing our finances into the spiritual realm. Tithes and Offerings therefore are often removed from the acronym. Our finances will primarily be spent on things that bring immediate gratification. Paying Bills on time, Debt reduction, Savings, and Investments, are therefore frequently removed from the acronym. That leaves two very selfish letters—M.E. We Maintain our household with food and the basic necessities, and we Enjoy life by purchasing those things that we think will bring us happiness. Looking out for M.E. may sound like a great idea, but we'll eventually find ourselves in a very miserable situation.

Repent and review

When we make money a source, it will always evade us. **Luke 16:13** says, "No servant can serve two masters…." No servant can serve both Source and resource. We've got to decide, by our actions, that God truly is the Source in our lives. If we don't, we'll continually grapple with limited resources. Our faith will waver and we will doubt God as our Source when we really never gave Him a chance.

If at least some of our money is not springing up again, then the first "re" that we need to do is to repent. Repentance is needed, because if we have not invested into the kingdom or other worthy endeavors, we have turned God's resource into a temporary source that only fulfills a short-term purpose and then dies.

If our money isn't springing up again, the second "re" that we need to do is to review. We need to review what's going on with our income. In addition to supporting our local church financially, we should be able to save a little money regularly to invest in our dream or a business venture of some type that will eventually cause our money to spring up again. The "re" that we are looking for from our resources, however, is not always going to come from some great investment opportunity or product idea. Investing in a $9 water detector that alerts you when there is a flood in your bathroom may save you hundreds in insurance deductibles. That is definitely getting "re" from your resources. Large or small, when we don't do these types of things, our resources get away from us and we tend to look at our employer and paycheck as the source instead of God.

Life Speaks

"We promise" were the last words Darren and Nicole tearfully spoke to Nicole's father before he passed away. Nicole had been raised in a godly household and her father, whom Darren admired, was instrumental in leading Darren to Christ. Pops, as they affectionately called him, knew that the couple had not been active in church.

He informed them that they would greatly benefit from getting involved with their church in some capacity whether great or small. This would help to add balance to their lives, break up the tunnel vision they had with their business, and begin the process of reconnecting them to the true Source, which is God. Once again, as he had always done with such grace and influence, Pops had spoken.

Why should I give to the Source?

[1] Give unto the LORD, O you mighty ones, Give unto the LORD glory and strength.
[2] Give unto the LORD the glory due to His name; Worship the LORD in the beauty of

holiness. [11] The LORD will give strength to His people; The LORD will bless His people with peace.

—David wrote in Psalms 29:1,2,11 (NKJV)

If God is the all-sufficient Source, then why do we need to give Him anything? Our giving back to God shows that we are still connected to the Source. It becomes a witness to others when they see or hear us speak of the continuous cycle of blessing and reverence that flows between God and His children.

In verse one of this passage the mighty are told to give. Often when people obtain a certain level of success, they feel they are the source and don't need God. Giving back to God is a way of humbling ourselves and remembering that we have not always been as blessed as we might be now. It keeps us from developing the foolish mindset that we are the source. Verse two indicates that what we give to God is due Him. God is the ultimate Source, and since He has blessed us with the resources to live our lives, we owe it to Him to give back.

Whether we have more money than we know what to do with or not enough to make ends meet, if we have made money our source we will not have peace. When people think of return on investment, many think only of money. But two of the greatest returns on investing in God as our Source cannot be measured by any currency. As verse eleven indicates, God gives us strength to endure and persevere. This includes weathering the financial storms of life. God also gives us peace so we don't have to worry about those storms.

With strength and peace, our minds are less cluttered and we are able to more clearly hear from God concerning our resources. We therefore greatly increase the probability that the financial decisions we make improve our position instead of making it worse.

Life Speaks

Everyone was pleasantly surprised when Darren and Nicole joined the Thursday night cell group. They were known as the "nice rich couple" who were too busy to get involved in the church. Once they were comfortably a part of the group, Nicole revealed that both she and Darren were youth group leaders in their previous church. They had been sidetracked by their business opportunity and just did not become active in church once they moved; now it was time to reconnect.

> Everyone in the group had average incomes and was of the opinion that people of substantial financial means couldn't be serious about God. Over the next few months the Carters helped to dismiss that perception.

Priming the pump

God disqualified David from building the temple because of his sin of sleeping with Bathsheba and then ordering her husband, Uriah, killed. That, however, didn't stop David from securing the resources for the temple that his son Solomon would construct. David and his people were excited about the project and willingly offered materials for the temple. Here is David's response to what he and the congregation were able to do:

> [10] David praised the LORD in the presence of the whole assembly, saying, "Praise be to you, O LORD, God of our father Israel, from everlasting to everlasting. [11] Yours, O LORD, is the greatness and the power and the glory and the majesty and the splendor, for everything in heaven and earth is yours. Yours, O LORD, is the kingdom; you are exalted as head over all. [12] Wealth and honor come from you; you are the ruler of all things. In your hands are strength and power to exalt and give strength to all. [13] Now, our God, we give you thanks, and praise your glorious name. [14] "But who am I, and who are my people, that we should be able to give as generously as this? Everything comes from you, and we have given you only what comes from your hand.
>
> —1 Chronicles 29:10-14

David shows us the proper attitude regarding source and resource. He acknowledges God as the ultimate Source of everything, and he speaks of the resources that come from Him. David didn't say, "I am the mighty king, look at the great kingdom I have created." He humbly recognizes that he is not worthy to receive or even give back to God. He acknowledges that all resources come from God, the Source. We simply give them back.

The issue is not about how much money we make. It's all about God. When we fully comprehend this, we will be delighted to give resources back to the Source. This giving back is like being on a farm with no running water. You can't just walk up to a pump and start pumping it and expect water to come out. The pump has to first be primed by pouring a little water into it. Once the pump is primed, water begins to flow out.

Spiritually if we don't embrace this concept, we'll think everything is about the money we can bring in. We'll be selfish in our giving. We'll squander the water that is designated for priming the pump. We'll make the mistake of making money our source.

Life Speaks

After hearing the testimonies in their cell group of the financial sacrifices others were making to keep Grace Fellowship going, Darren and Nicole felt convicted to begin giving. A week after their first offering they received a phone call from Deacon Oliver, head of the finance committee, requesting a meeting with them. Their initial thought was the church was going to ask them for more money.

In the meeting, however, Deacon Oliver informed them that he had been praying about what company to select to provide marketing support for his business. When he saw their offering check with their business name on it he wanted to find out more about the Carters' business. It wasn't a huge offering they gave, but it blessed the church, became the answer to someone else's prayer, primed the pump, and provided a new client for Marketing Solutions.

Loving the Source

Paul, in his letter to Timothy, speaks of those who foolishly make money their source in an attempt to become rich.

> [10] For the love of money is a root of all kinds of evil. Some people, eager for money, have wandered from the faith and pierced themselves with many griefs.
>
> —1 Timothy 6:10

Look at this verse and substitute the word "resources" for the word "money" and the word "Source" for the word "faith." It should become clear that loving our resources puts us in a worse relationship with the Source. Conversely, loving the Source puts us in a better relationship with our resources.

The resource is tangible and is therefore coveted more than the Source. But as this verse indicates, loving the resource of money doesn't only cause financial problems. This illicit love affair is an open invitation to all types of other evil being introduced into our lives. We must love the Source and He will instruct us on the proper use of the resources so that we are generating blessings that bring joy instead of curses that bring grief.

Yes, yes, and maybe

22 The blessing of the LORD makes one rich, And He adds no sorrow with it.

—Proverbs 10:22 (NKJV)

The blessings or resources of God, the Source, bring wealth without sorrow. Is there generally turmoil associated with your finances? The more financial woes we have, the greater the likelihood that we have been confused between source and resource.

Does that mean once we understand and apply the concepts of source and resource we'll be rich? Yes, yes, and maybe. The first yes means that by focusing on the Source, we will be so in tune with God that we will be rich in spirit and the lack of resource will stress us out less. The second yes requires an understanding of the definition of the word "rich." Rich doesn't always imply that we will be millionaires. Rich means that we will be accumulating wealth. Our assets, over time, will outweigh our liabilities. So yes, we will be rich because rich simply means having more than enough, having an abundance, being well supplied.

The "maybe" comes into play because being rich, as in a millionaire, depends on how much "re" we have in our resources. If we spend more as we make more, trying to appear wealthy before we actually are, that "maybe" turns into a no. But as we find ways to make money spring up again, one day we might just become millionaires!

Being a millionaire is one thing, but if our reason for wanting wealth is primarily for personal pleasure, then we are out of line with why God would allow us to have wealth. God is not impressed by our telling Him that if He gave us a million dollars we would tithe. Tithing is something we should be striving to do at every financial level. God wants to know what we would do with the other 90 percent.

After giving tithes and offerings, what would we do with our riches? Would we use them wisely? Would we use them in a way that makes them multiply? Would we make them a true resource where they would spring up again? Would people see our good works and glorify God? We need to understand the reason that God our Source gives us the resource of money.

In his letter to the church at Corinth, Paul reminds the Corinthians of God's faithfulness and the purpose for their giving of resources for the work of the kingdom.

[8] And God is able to make all grace (every favor and earthly blessing) come to you in abundance, so that you may always and under all circumstances and whatever the need be self-sufficient [possessing enough to require no aid or support and furnished in abundance for every good work and charitable donation].

—2 Corinthians 9:8 (AMP)

The Source is able to make resources come to us in abundance. Why? So that we will always have enough of what we need and can spend the extra on every good work, building the kingdom. What do we do with extra money? Is it going to every good restaurant, every good sale, every good movie, every good deal? Sometimes that's okay because having all sufficiency doesn't mean that we have just the bare minimum and only spend the extra on the kingdom. But, we should possess the discernment to know when our extra spending is out of alignment with the will of God. This discernment is developed by prayerfully considering every purchase we make and thereby inviting God into the process.

Life Speaks

Business travel, personal travel, it all was an enjoyable part of the lifestyle of Darren and Nicole. Their church involvement was beginning to pick up, however, and they were connecting with more people in the congregation. They were starting to feel a spiritual void when they were away. A trip to Hawaii was scheduled in four months that would be a combination anniversary/business trip—they wouldn't miss it for the world.

When the pastor stood up in church on Sunday and mentioned that the church was $1900 short of what was needed for the youth mission trip, Darren and Nicole looked at each other, smiled, and at the same time said, "Bermuda!" The amount of $1900 was the exact amount they were getting ready to mail for a different trip to Bermuda the following summer. God had spoken to both of them. The trip to Bermuda was cancelled and the youth mission trip would receive the funding it needed.

When we neglect the Source, we become dependent on manna to sustain us. Manna, however, will never satisfy us.

In addition to lacking in variety, manna is designed only to meet short-term immediate needs. We need resources that extend beyond the situation at hand. For this reason we must first seek the Source and His righteousness and all the resources will be added to us.

Unit Review

1. Do you believe that God is the Source and money is only a resource? If so, how do you demonstrate this in handling your finances?

    _____

    _____

    _____

    _____

    _____

2. What are some ways that you currently receive some positive "re" from your resources?

    _____

    _____

    _____

    _____

    _____

3. If your money is not springing up again in your life, the first two "re's" that you need to do are _____ and _____.

4. Since God is the endless Source, why does Psalms 29:1,2,11 instruct us to give to Him?

    _____

    _____

    _____

    _____

5. Can you summarize David's perception of God as the Source in 1 Chronicles 29:10-14?

    _____

    _____

    _____

    _____

6. Review 1 Timothy 6:10. What percentage of your grief stems from your use of money? How can applying the concept of source and resource relieve you of this grief?

    _____

    _____

    _____

    _____

7. According to Proverbs 10:22, the blessings of the Lord are designed to make us rich. What are three meanings of the word "rich"?

    _____

    _____

    _____

    _____

8. If we want to be monetarily rich, and if according to 2 Corinthians 9:8 God is able to do this for us, what might be the delay?

    _____

    _____

    _____

9. If you believe Jesus was resurrected from the dead, do you believe it is any more difficult for Him to raise your finances out of the T.O.M.B.? If you are a candidate for the T.O.M.B., what's keeping you from going in?

_____

_____

_____

10. Darren and Nicole were fortunate to have someone in their lives to give them spiritual guidance. What can we do to help other Christians who may be off track because they don't understand the concept of source and resource?

_____

_____

_____

11. What, if any, revelation has God spoken to you from this unit?

_____

_____

_____

12. What action items can you develop to apply the concepts of this unit?
Action Item #1:

_____

_____

Action Item #2:

_____

_____

Unit Jewel:

Being led by the Source puts us in a better relationship with our resources. Being led by our resources puts us in a worse relationship with the Source.

Unit Summary:

Being able to maintain the distinction of God as our Source, and money as a resource, is foundational to walking in the abundance of God's provision.

Meditation/Prayer Focus:

And my God will meet all your needs according to his glorious riches in Christ Jesus.
—Philippians 4:19

It is God, not riches, who meets my needs. He is the Source who supplies me with resources based on His riches.

Struggle Class

Life Speaks: Marcus and Jennifer Anderson

Marcus and Jennifer Anderson had no regrets about Jennifer staying home with the two boys until they were of school age. Things often got tight financially, but they managed. When Jennifer returned to her job as a computer technician, she and Marcus knew their financial problems were solved. That's what they thought until the debt began to pile up and their dinner conversations began to once again revolve around the same stressful topic of money.

If God is not our Source, and if there is no "re" in our resources, then we're among the masses in the lower, middle, and upper classes who form the "Struggle Class." It doesn't matter how much money we make. If we're always stretched and stressed over money, we're in Struggle Class.

To get out of Struggle Class we must trust the Source and do the right things with our resources. Remember, when we're in Struggle Class we're failing God if we're not giving tithes and offerings; we're failing our families if we're not providing for their needs; and we're failing our creditors if we're not meeting our obligations. If we're tired of failing we have to flee from Struggle Class. This exodus will help us develop discipline, resurrect our financial position, and reestablish credibility with God, our families, and our creditors.

Stop struggling

Matthew 5:38-48 records a portion of Jesus' sermon on the mount in which He instructs us to stop struggling.

[38] "You have heard that it was said, 'Eye for eye, and tooth for tooth.' [39] But I tell you, Do not resist an evil person. If someone strikes you on the right cheek, turn to him the other also. [40] And if someone wants to sue you and take your tunic, let him have your cloak as well. [41] If someone forces you to go one mile, go with him two miles. [42] Give to the one who asks you, and do not turn away from the one who wants to borrow from you. [43] "You have heard that it was said, 'Love your neighbor and hate your enemy.' [44] But I tell you: Love your enemies and pray for those who persecute you, [45] that you may be sons of your Father in heaven. He causes his sun to rise on the evil and the good, and sends rain on the righteous and the unrighteous. [46] If you love those who love you, what reward will you get? Are not even the tax collectors doing that? [47] And if you greet only your brothers, what are you doing more than others? Do not even pagans do that? [48] Be perfect, therefore, as your heavenly Father is perfect.

If God is going to be able to most effectively use us for His glory, we must understand that worldly tactics, such as struggling, cannot be used to accomplish kingdom objectives. As these verses point out, struggling is very common. Jesus, however, starts verses 39 and 44 with a key word—"but." We are called to take something that is very common, struggling, and make it uncommon to us. Why? As children of God we are not supposed to be in Struggle Class with the rest of the world!

Think about why we struggle over things. Why do kids fight over toys? Why do nations war over territory? Why do people battle over any and everything? It's called supply and demand. It's all about what we perceive to be limited resources. God is trying to teach us that His resources are unlimited and if we really trust Him as our Source, He will take care of us. God has the supply to meet every demand.

Struggle takes our minds off the Source and puts them on the failing resource. We are then defeated when we see our money depleted. We struggle because we view money as a source and not a resource that God can and will replenish.

Verse 48 reminds us that as we mature we'll understand that children of the Source should not be struggling over resources. When we stop struggling, not only do we get out of Struggle Class, but we become a powerful witness to others in the process.

> ### *Life Speaks*
>
> Marcus and Jennifer agreed that they would resign their positions in the choir and as Sunday school teachers until they could adjust to the transition of being a two-income household. After all, their new time commitment would be challenging to say the least and wouldn't allow for rehearsals and lesson preparations.
>
> Purchasing two new cars and a new house in the first three months of Jennifer's returning to work was just the start. Eating out almost every night, weekend family getaways, and lavish personal purchases took their toll, not only on their time, but their finances and energy.
>
> This particular weekend the Andersons were staying in town. It would be their first time going to church in almost two months. They were beginning to feel a little out of sync with church and were planning to give an offering on Sunday. Marcus took out the checkbook, stared at it for a moment, and slumped back onto the couch. Jennifer was all too familiar with his body language. The question for the evening, "How could we afford to tithe on one income and now struggle to give an offering when we have two incomes?"

The five-stage pattern of Struggle Class

In Luke 15:11-18 Jesus gives the parable of the Prodigal Son, which we will use to outline the five-stage pattern of Struggle Class.

[11] Jesus continued: "There was a man who had two sons. [12] The younger one said to his father, 'Father, give me my share of the estate.' So he divided his property between them. [13] "Not long after that, the younger son got together all he had, set off for a distant country and there squandered his wealth in wild living. [14] After he had spent everything, there was a severe famine in that whole country, and he began to be in need. [15] So he went and hired himself out to a citizen of that country, who sent him to his fields to feed pigs. [16] He longed to fill his stomach with the pods that the pigs were eating, but no one gave him anything. [17] "When he came to his senses, he said, 'How many of my father's hired men have food to spare, and here I am starving to death! [18] I will set out and go back to my father and say to him: Father, I have sinned against heaven and against you.

Most people in Struggle Class go through the following five stages.

Stage 1: In verse 12 the young man says, "Forget the Source; just give me the resources! I don't need authority over me; just give me enough money and I'll be all right!" This stage is called Alienation.

Stage 2: In verse 13 the young man wastes his resources. This stage is called Deterioration. In this stage, you find out that the resources you had didn't last as long or go as far as you thought they would.

Stage 3: In verses 14-16 the young man is struggling. He'll do anything to get more of the resources he needs. This stage is called Desperation.

Struggle Class is full of people who are caught in a vicious cycle between stages 1-3. They continually alienate themselves from God, and every time they get a breakthrough it quickly deteriorates. Then they become desperate and begin to make unwise financial decisions. People caught in this cycle constantly talk about the next raise, promotion, or breakthrough.

Alienation, Deterioration, and then Desperation: The first letters of those three words make the acronym A.D.D. (Attention Deficit Disorder). It's as if God is saying, "My child, can I get your attention? You are running in circles, sinking in despair and your ways are not working. If I could just keep your attention long enough, I can erase the deficit in your life and turn the disorder into order."

Stage 4: In verses 17-19 the young man is maturing. He begins to understand that his Source is greater than the resources he wasted. Likewise, we, too, must understand just how mighty our Source is. Life is not about the resources we have at hand, but the Source that we keep close to our hearts. This stage is called Realization. In the Realization stage you simply start paying attention. You make an assessment of what is most important in life. The line between wants and needs becomes clearly defined and is reflected in your revised actions.

Stage 5: In verse 20 the young man decides to return to the Source. This stage is called Restoration. The restoration stage is characterized by renewed spiritual vitality with an emphasis on giving to the kingdom.

Getting out of Struggle Class means admitting that you have A.D.D. You're alienated from God, your resources are deteriorating, and you're desperate! You have to believe that there is a cure. You have to tell yourself that you want to be a child prodigy and not a prodigal child. You have to go on to stage 4, which is Realization, and then to stage 5 which is Restoration with our Father God.

> ### *Life Speaks*
>
> Nothing had changed; Pastor Jeff's office looked the same as it did seven years ago when Marcus and Jennifer were there for pre-marital counseling. Once again they left with a game plan. It was a humbling experience but they knew exactly what they needed to do.
>
> They had moved from a rented two-bedroom townhouse into a mortgaged five-bedroom dream house. They now had to find something in the middle. They sold one of their new cars and got a very reliable four-year-old used car. They got on a budget that allowed Jennifer to work part-time, yet allowed for some family entertainment. Finally, Marcus and Jennifer got back in the choir, the Sunday school teacher rotation, and they started tithing again.
>
> All the extra money had brought much excitement into the Andersons' lives, but it stole their happiness. It was fun at first, but it wasn't worth the strain that it placed on their relationship with each other and with God.

The embarrassment of Struggle Class

In 1 Corinthians 6:1-7 Paul expresses his disappointment with the Corinthians for being in Struggle Class and embarrassing the kingdom.

> [1] If any of you has a dispute with another, dare he take it before the ungodly for judgment instead of before the saints? [2] Do you not know that the saints will judge the world? And if you are to judge the world, are you not competent to judge trivial cases? [3] Do you not know that we will judge angels? How much more the things of this life! [4] Therefore, if you have disputes about such matters, appoint as judges even men of little account in the church! [5] I say this to shame you. Is it possible that there is nobody among you wise enough to judge a dispute between believers? [6] But instead, one brother goes to law against another—and this in front of unbelievers! [7] The very fact that you have lawsuits among you means you have been completely defeated already. Why not rather be wronged? Why not rather be cheated?

When you are in Struggle Class, it's just a matter of time before you will be struggling not only with money but with other people. Paul told the Corinthians that when

Christians start struggling with each other as the rest of the world does, we embarrass God. In verse 7 Paul asked, "Why don't you just let the offense go?" To get out of Struggle Class we have to learn which battles are worth fighting and which are not.

It's one thing if a non-believer takes us to court or if we feel we have to take a non-believer to court. To sue or not to sue is going to be a personal decision based on the circumstances, our faith, and our Christian maturity. But in this case, Paul was talking about Christians prosecuting other Christians.

The second way we embarrass God is by taking our struggles out of God's court and into the world's court. The church is supposed to function as a governing authority in the affairs of its people. We will remain in Struggle Class if we only go to church leadership for advice, but go to a worldly judge for the final ruling. We will remain in Struggle Class if we are quicker to say, "I need to get a good lawyer!" than we are to say, "I need to find godly counsel."

Struggle Class remains a reality if we feel there is no one in the body of Christ who can make a better ruling in our circumstances than a secular court system. Struggle Class, however, becomes a thing of the past when we return to our respect for the church. If a judge threatens the average person with jail time, actions are usually corrected. If a pastor attempts to call a member into accountability, that member might just look for a new church. If a judge requires the average person to pay restitution, the person pays it. If a pastor mentions giving tithes and offerings, some say, "God understands if I don't."

If Christians don't respect the church, why should the world? Is it any wonder that we remain in Struggle Class? We wouldn't walk into a court date late. We wouldn't tell the judge, "I was tired and I couldn't make it to court", not if we wanted a favorable ruling. Therefore we should not do these things to God and expect Him to give us a favorable ruling and deliver us from Struggle Class.

Struggle Class is the embarrassing result of not trusting God, our Source, or His system. It is a result of fearing man more than we fear God. Malachi 1:6-14 further addresses this issue.

[6] "A son honors his father, and a servant his master. If I am a father, where is the honor due me? If I am a master, where is the respect due me?" says the LORD Almighty. "It is you, O priests, who show contempt for my name. "But you ask, 'How have we shown contempt for your name?' [7] "You place defiled food on my altar. "But you ask, 'How have we defiled you?' "By saying that the LORD's table is contemptible. [8] When you bring blind

animals for sacrifice, is that not wrong? When you sacrifice crippled or diseased animals, is that not wrong? Try offering them to your governor! Would he be pleased with you? Would he accept you?" says the LORD Almighty. [9] "Now implore God to be gracious to us. With such offerings from your hands, will he accept you?"-says the LORD Almighty. [10] "Oh, that one of you would shut the temple doors, so that you would not light useless fires on my altar! I am not pleased with you," says the LORD Almighty, "and I will accept no offering from your hands. [11] My name will be great among the nations, from the rising to the setting of the sun. In every place incense and pure offerings will be brought to my name, because my name will be great among the nations," says the LORD Almighty. [12] "But you profane it by saying of the Lord's table, 'It is defiled,' and of its food, 'It is contemptible.' [13] And you say, 'What a burden!' and you sniff at it contemptuously," says the LORD Almighty. "When you bring injured, crippled or diseased animals and offer them as sacrifices, should I accept them from your hands?" says the LORD . [14] "Cursed is the cheat who has an acceptable male in his flock and vows to give it, but then sacrifices a blemished animal to the Lord. For I am a great king," says the LORD Almighty, "and my name is to be feared among the nations.

—Malachi 1:6-14

In verses 6-10 God asked, "Where is my honor?" Surely we should honor God more than the legal system or an employer, but unfortunately this is not always the case. By our lifestyle the unsaved world should know that we serve a great God. They should be lining up to find out about our God. This doesn't happen if we remain in Struggle Class.

As verse 13 implies, why do Christians always talk about how church drains them? Why is church often such a struggle? It's not supposed to be that way. Verse 14 explains it for us. We bring a curse on ourselves when we have what God asks of us but choose to give something less than our best. With that curse comes a struggle that is not only embarrassing to us, but also to the kingdom.

Decrease your struggle and increase your witness

Sometimes we unintentionally embarrass the kingdom trying not to embarrass ourselves. In an effort to save face we often demand our rights rather than walking in the righteousness of God. In the following verses Isaac exhibits the humility and faith that goes a long way in increasing our witness to unbelievers.

¹ Now there was a famine in the land—besides the earlier famine of Abraham's time-and Isaac went to Abimelech king of the Philistines in Gerar. ² The LORD appeared to Isaac and said, "Do not go down to Egypt; live in the land where I tell you to live. ³ Stay in this land for a while, and I will be with you and will bless you. For to you and your descendants I will give all these lands and will confirm the oath I swore to your father Abraham. ¹² Isaac planted crops in that land and the same year reaped a hundredfold, because the LORD blessed him.

—Genesis 26:1-3,12

God told Isaac that the land and the countries belonged to Abraham's children. The Source supplied the resource. Isaac moved in, sowed the land, and it prospered greatly. He got some "re" out of his resources, and he became rich.

¹⁶ Then Abimelech said to Isaac, "Move away from us; you have become too powerful for us." ¹⁷ So Isaac moved away from there and encamped in the Valley of Gerar and settled there.

—Genesis 26:16-17

God said the land belonged to Isaac. Isaac worked the land and became rich and mightier than King Abimelech. It would seem that the king needed to be the one leaving! But what did Isaac do? He left! What about his investment in the land? How could he just walk away from all of his hard work? Either Isaac wasn't too bright, was afraid, or he had great confidence in his Source that provided his resources.

¹⁸ Isaac reopened the wells that had been dug in the time of his father Abraham, which the Philistines had stopped up after Abraham died, and he gave them the same names his father had given them. ¹⁹ Isaac's servants dug in the valley and discovered a well of fresh water there. ²⁰ But the herdsmen of Gerar quarreled with Isaac's herdsmen and said, "The water is ours!" So he named the well Esek, because they disputed with him. ²¹ Then they dug another well, but they quarreled over that one also; so he named it Sitnah. ²² He moved on from there and dug another well, and no one quarreled over it. He named it Rehoboth, saying, "Now the LORD has given us room and we will flourish in the land."

—Genesis 26:18-22

Isaac had his servants dig a well and the herdsmen of Gerar wanted to fight over it. Isaac let them have it. Isaac had another well dug and again the herdsmen of Gerar wanted to battle over it. Isaac let them have that one, too. He had yet another well dug and they finally left him alone. Why didn't Isaac stand up for what was his? Isaac understood that his Source was much bigger than his resources. He understood that life is not always about struggling with one foe after another.

We have to understand that the enemy is not flesh and blood. It's not our job to destroy the enemy. We want to convert people. We should care more about witnessing to others and seeing them saved than we care about demanding our rights. Jesus had a right not to die, but He died. He didn't struggle. He gave up His rights and died showing us that we don't have to struggle the way we do.

Life Speaks

Jennifer couldn't have been happier, and it showed. She was back to work in a part-time job that she enjoyed, but more importantly, her family and spiritual life were back on track. As Cynthia approached her on Monday morning, Jennifer immediately sensed something was wrong. In the past, Cynthia had gone out of her way to make it known that she ran the office. There was always a not-so-subtle cutthroat competitiveness about her that was missing today. Cynthia was barely able to pull Jennifer into an empty conference room before breaking down in to tears.

Cynthia had been diagnosed with breast cancer. As a breast cancer survivor, Jennifer knew exactly what Cynthia was up against and invited Cynthia to join a cancer support group at her church. Cynthia accepted the invitation and one month later also accepted the invitation to give her life to Christ.

[26]Meanwhile, Abimelech had come to him from Gerar, with Ahuzzath his personal adviser and Phicol the commander of his forces. [27]Isaac asked them, "Why have you come to me, since you were hostile to me and sent me away?" [28]They answered, "We saw clearly that the LORD was with you; so we said, 'There ought to be a sworn agreement between us'—between us and you. Let us make a treaty with you [29]that you will do us no harm, just as we did not molest you but always treated you well and sent you away in peace. And now you are blessed by the LORD."

—Genesis 26:26-29

Abimelech and company saw God in Isaac and wanted to make a covenant with him. Getting out of Struggle Class is not just about us. It's about the business of the kingdom. The world doesn't need to see us always struggling like them and with them. The world needs to see us blessed of the Lord. Let us vow to do whatever we must do to get out of Struggle Class. When we do, the quality of our life will improve along with the effectiveness of our witness to a struggling world.

Manna fell at night, was gathered in the day, could be collected only in small quantities, and with the exception of the day before the Sabbath, could not be kept overnight. Few things cause struggles more than limitations and restrictions placed on us. Confinement either motivates us to be free or encourages us to accept our struggles as being normal. What choice will you make?

Unit Review

1. As Christians we are to produce disciples. How is this made more difficult if we are in Struggle Class?

   _____

   _____

   _____

   _____

   _____

2. Name the three entities that you reestablish credibility with when you get out of Struggle Class.

   _____

   _____

   _____

   _____

   _____

3. T/F _____ God can most effectively use you when you are in Struggle Class.

   T/F _____ If God is going to be able to use you at all in Struggle Class, you cannot use worldly tactics to accomplish kingdom objectives.

   T/F _____ The perception of limited resources is what keeps us in Struggle Class.

4. Circle the following words that are not part of the five-stage pattern of Struggle Class.

Alienation	Anticipation	Deterioration	Desperation
Procrastination	Restoration	Realization	

5. In what ways is our being in Struggle Class an embarrassment to God?

_____

_____

_____

_____

6. Why did Isaac repeatedly surrender resources that were rightfully his?

_____

_____

_____

_____

7. When you think of Isaac's actions, the world might use words like "pushover" and "wimp" to describe him. Is it worth being called such names or thought about in this way if your actions bring deliverance from Struggle Class?

_____

_____

_____

_____

8. What happened to Isaac's witness as a result of his not being in Struggle Class?

_____

_____

_____

_____

9. Marcus and Jennifer had to learn the hard way about the harsh realities of Struggle Class. Can you identify spiritually-mature Christians who don't appear to be in Struggle Class? If so, list their names.

_____

_____

_____

If you are in Struggle Class, prayerfully consider counseling with someone on this list prior to making major financial decisions.

10. What, if any, revelation has God spoken to you from this unit?

_____

_____

_____

_____

11. What action items can you develop to apply the concepts of this unit?

Action Item #1:

_____

_____

_____

Action Item #2:

_____

_____

_____

Unit Jewel:

Life is not about the resources we have at hand, but the Source we keep close to our hearts. When we decrease our struggle, we increase our witness.

Unit Summary:

Struggle Class will welcome us no matter what our level of income. God can do the most through us, however, when we learn to cease from struggling.

Meditation/Prayer Focus:

Do not be afraid or discouraged… For the battle is not yours, but God's…. You will not have to fight this battle. Take up your positions; stand firm and see the deliverance the Lord will give you.

—2 Chronicles 20:15-17

Are you tired of the struggle? If so, take your financial positions and stand firm on them. What is your position on honoring God with your finances? What is your position on entertainment, fast food, and other potentially budget-breaking spending? Declare your positions before God in prayer and watch for His deliverance.

Then the Manna Ceased

Life Speaks: Pam Jordan

"Why did they have to go and change things!" Pam exclaimed angrily. "All we do is bust our butts around here while they take more benefits from us!" Pam was responding to the new policy of her company to no longer give employees an annual cost-of-living adjustment. The company was struggling with its third straight year of declining profits. The executive office felt it best to implement a performance-based system that would move the company forward and potentially provide even greater pay increases for the employees.

The cost-of-living adjustment wasn't much, but at least it was something that could be depended on regularly. To the employees it was better than nothing, but it was not helping the company to meet its goals. It was time for a change. The manna had ceased.

God fed his people manna when they were wandering around in the wilderness of Sinai. Manna was food that was white, small, and round in appearance. It was called the bread or corn of heaven, and angel food. Nobody had to work for it; it just fell out of the sky every night. All they had to do was scoop it up in the morning.

Today we are still captivated with the idea of God dropping blessings out of the sky. After all, God is no respecter of persons, and if He did it once, then surely He can do it again. As much as we would like for God to rain blessings from heaven, we need to understand that while God still performs miracles, we don't hear reports of them falling out of the sky.

Why manna then and not now?

God graciously provided manna for His people and fed them for forty years. Why? The obvious answer would be because they were hungry. Exodus 16:7,12 tells us another side of the story.

> [7] and in the morning you will see the glory of the LORD, because he has heard your grumbling against him. Who are we, that you should grumble against us?" [12] "I have heard the grumbling of the Israelites. Tell them, 'At twilight you will eat meat, and in the morning you will be filled with bread. Then you will know that I am the LORD your God.' "

God was tired of the ingratitude of the Israelites. The Israelites did not believe that they would survive the wilderness under the leadership of Moses and they made his job extremely difficult. Manna, therefore, was sent to stop their grumbling. The good news for the Israelites was that God was on a mission to send Jesus through their lineage. God wasn't going to let anything, not even a rebellious people, keep Jesus from coming.

Jesus' mission, however, is now completed. Sometimes God still blesses us when we haven't measured up, but the bad news for us is that He probably is not going to perform miracles for us just because we throw a tantrum like the Israelites.

Where do you want to eat?

The children of Israel ate in three different places.

- Place #1: Egypt. Egypt represents the unsaved world of sin and bondage. There was a limited variety of basic food, but there was plenty to eat. The people were slaves.

- Place #2: The Wilderness. The wilderness represents coming out of sin and following God, but then becoming disobedient when the going gets rough. The food was miraculously provided daily, but it was rationed. It was nutritious, but the same every day. The people were wandering in the wilderness.
- Place #3: The Promised Land. The Promised Land represents walking in obedience and faith in God. The food was the best life had to offer and abounded in quality, quantity, and variety. The people had battles with various enemies, but they were victorious and free.

Most would agree that the Promised Land would be the best place to eat, but the children of Israel wanted to go back to the familiarity of Egypt. They didn't mind being enslaved and abused as long as life was predictable. Today, if we are so set on seeing miracles without changing our ways, does that mean we really don't mind the wilderness that we are going through as much as we say we do? Do we want manna to be our main form of blessing? Are we heading back to the routine of the world and away from the exciting unknown that God has for us? If we are hoping for miracles so we don't have to change our ways, we are only extending our stay in the wilderness and delaying our arrival in the Promised Land.

The children of Israel were miraculously blessed in the wilderness. It was a miracle that their shoes and clothes didn't wear out. It was a miracle that God gave water from a rock so the water didn't run out. It was a miracle that God provided manna and their food didn't run out. What they didn't understand was that their lives were running out.

Their lives were going nowhere but in circles. It was the same frustrating scenario every day. They were dying for miracles and they were dying with miracles. That's not the life that we want. If we therefore have the manna mentality, in which we murmur and idly wait on God for another miracle, then that must cease. We have to walk by faith and obedience in order to get out of the wilderness and into the Promised Land.

What could be better than a miracle?

The day after the Israelites ate food from the Promised Land, the manna ceased. This was not symbolic of the end of miracles, but of a new era in which God's people exercised their faith and saw even more miraculous things happen. Not only did the Israelites experience a variety of food; they also were getting ready to see God work in a multitude of ways in their lives as they walked in obedience. The children of Israel learned a lesson that we can learn as well. Regularly walking in faith and obedience brings far greater blessings than the daily miracle of manna.

There were plenty of unknowns, not to mention known enemies awaiting the Israelites in the Promised Land. Therefore they chose to gather manna daily rather than to obey and go forward by faith. They found it more convenient to let God take care of them in the wilderness than to trust Him and receive their inheritance.

There was no personal relationship between the Israelites and God. If you don't have God internally, you always have to look for Him externally. You feel you have to see the manna. When you don't have faith, sight is required. Because of this lack of personal relationship, either staying in the wilderness or returning to Egypt were both seen as better options to the Israelites than going into the Promised Land.

John 14:10-12 records Jesus saying that God was in Him and He was in God. That's a personal relationship. Then He said those who believed on Him would do greater works than He did. That's miraculous. This is possible because when Jesus went to the Father, He sent back the Holy Spirit to dwell within us. Again, that's a personal relationship. When it comes to all the great things He was known for, Jesus made it clear that it was the Father within Him who did the work. God works greatly through us when He dwells richly in us. What could be better than a miracle?—a miracle in which God works through us to bring it to pass.

Life Speaks

"We can complain or we can comply! You're acting like this company has never done anything for us. Even without the cost-of-living adjustment, name one company that pays a better salary. Name one company that has better benefits. Name one company that has taken more strides to ensure that no employee is laid off. Instead of looking at what's being taken away, look at what is being offered. Today you work for this company and now they are asking you to work with them to make sure we all have jobs five years from now. I know each of you, and I know that individually and as a team we have the talent to meet and exceed the performance goals the company has set. Now quit acting like it's the end of the world!

Open your eyes and see the horizon of possibility before us. By next week I want you to present me with ways that we are going to meet this challenge. That's all I have for today."

It was a short and somber meeting. The message from Juan, the team manager, was quite direct. Juan was well liked and respected and had a way of bringing the needed perspective. He was right. And before the big announcement many of us were even complaining about how boring and dull our jobs had become. Once again, me, "Ms. big mouth Pam," thought I spoke for all. I sent an email to Juan and the unit apologizing for my outburst. How easily I had forgotten that I had been praying to God for much-needed change on the job. God answered my prayer! Juan wanted ideas by next week. He would have mine by the end of this week.

Miracles vs works

Many people, if given the choice between miracles falling from the sky and having to work, would choose the miracles. Isn't it ironic that Jesus used the word "works" more so than the word "miracle" to describe what He did? Jesus only used the word "miracle" twice in the Bible and both times it referred to man's viewpoint. Jesus called them works, man called them miracles. The miracle is always in the eye of the beholder.

When we look at famous athletes, we often view the plays they make as miraculous. But they see what they do as another day on the job. This is what they have focused on, devoted their lives to, and worked hard to achieve. It's not a miracle to them. It just looks miraculous to us. They paid their dues and now they are in the Promised Land of their professions. If they had waited for manna to fall and bless them, they wouldn't be where they are. Instead, they had a personal relationship with a dream deep inside them. When they embraced the dream, the results became quite obvious. What looks miraculous to us is just hard work and dedication to them.

That's precisely what God wants from us. If we can embrace the Spirit of God within us, the works that we do will look miraculous to others. That's exactly what Jesus did. Luke 10:17-20 describes the disciples being excited about their ability to cast out demons. It was a miracle! Jesus told them instead of getting excited about miracles, get excited that your names are written in heaven. Get excited about the wonderful blessings that come through a personal relationship working with God to meet kingdom objectives.

Life is not about one miracle after another. God is trying to get us from Egypt, through the wilderness and into the Promised Land. He used miracles to get us out of Egypt and through the wilderness. Now the manna has ceased. If we are to arrive in the Promised Land, we must show God the work we can do by walking in obedience.

Life Speaks

"Wow, Pam! How did you come up with that idea?" Juan asked. It was just announced that Pam was the recipient of the first company performance partnership award. Her idea to improve the inventory control system would save the company $20,000 a year. Pam couldn't believe her eyes. The check she received for just one idea was slightly more than her annual cost-of-living adjustment! Once Pam made the connection between the company's decision and God answering her prayer, she began to see how God was opening up a new door of opportunity for her. All she had to do was be willing and obedient to accept the change.

Why did God perform the miracle of manna?

When we think of any miracle, the reason we feel God performs it is to bless someone with something they need or want. While that may be true, there are reasons that God performs miracles that we don't explore very often. Why did God give the Israelites the miracle of manna? Deuteronomy 8:3 gives us some insight.

> ³ He humbled you, causing you to hunger and then feeding you with manna, which neither you nor your fathers had known, to teach you that man does not live on bread alone but on every word that comes from the mouth of the LORD.
>
> —Deuteronomy 8:3

God gave the Israelites manna to teach them. The Israelites thought they were going to leave Egypt and just dance right into the buffet line of the Promised Land. God, however, let their hunger get to the desperation point so they would understand that they needed His Word to survive. The manna or bread was a miracle. So you can look at this verse as saying man shall not live by miracles alone. We need less of the manna and more of the bread of life, which is the Word of God to survive. We can do nothing, let things get to a point of hopelessness in our lives, and then wait for a miracle. Or we can obey God's Word and trust Him to guide and take care of us.

> [16] He gave you manna to eat in the desert, something your fathers had never known, to humble and to test you so that in the end it might go well with you.
>
> —Deuteronomy 8:16

God gave the Israelites manna to humble them. When we think of miracles, we think of words like joy and excitement, but very rarely humility. But when a miracle is received we should take time to reflect on just how unworthy we are and how good God is. The children of Israel were not humbled by the daily miracle of manna. Instead of being humbled they became indignant. They were tired of manna, but instead of being excited about going forward to the Promised Land, they wanted to go backward into Egypt.

If we think about it, through technology, medicine, and scientific advancement, we live in an era of daily modern miracles. But as a society are we grateful to God and ready to go forward into all He has prepared for us? Or have we turned our backs on God? Despite His goodness, are we ready to return to the world of sin that He sent His Son to save us from?

Verse 16 also tells us that God gave the Israelites Manna to test them. It's easy to only see miracles as blessings and not as tests. We think of tribulations and trials as tests, but not miracles. We see a miracle as the thing that is going to make our lives complete and perfect. If a million dollars fell from the sky, we would feel our financial worries were over. The miracle of manna, however, was not given to make the Israelite's lives complete. After God taught, humbled, and tested them, He was still trying to take them somewhere—the Promised Land. God never intended for His people to get permanently hooked on the wilderness miracles, and that's why the manna had to cease.

If God would not have performed the miracle of manna, had He not allowed the trial of the wilderness, the children of Israel would have entered the Promised Land with the same mindset they had in Egypt. They would have still been confused between source and resource. They would have gone wild on the blessings and forgot who it was that blessed them. They would have started hoarding and fighting. They would have abused each other and probably developed the same type of oppressive system that they were delivered from. They would have returned to Struggle Class. God used the miracle of manna to train His people. He didn't allow them to erect barns so they could store the manna. Every day they had to go out and see that once again God had provided their daily bread.

When we are forced to lean and depend on God daily, it can be a humbling and proving experience. This experience will either cause us to go back to the world, strand us in the wilderness, or teach and prepare us to enter into the Promised Land.

When we live a life of faithless disobedience, we will always be looking for another miracle. We won't even realize that our attitude and actions have not changed since the last time God blessed us with a miracle.

Once the children of Israel made it to the Promised Land and ate of that land, the manna ceased. When you walk by faith and obedience, you don't need the miracle of manna. You are no longer hoping that God will drop something out of the sky.

By your faithfulness and obedience you will begin to see God's blessings all around you. Your confidence in God will increase, and your self-esteem will improve as you become productive and fruitful. Your works will be looked upon by others as miraculous because of God's orchestration. People will see your good works and glorify God. You will begin to see just how much of your life was wasted in the wilderness and you will be overjoyed that the manna has ceased.

Unit Review

1. God sent manna to stop the _____ of the children of Israel.

2. What would make Egypt and the wilderness a more appealing place to eat than the Promised Land?

   _____

   _____

   _____

   _____

   _____

3. T/F _____ The ceasing of the manna was symbolic of the end of miracles.

   T/F _____ We can only escape the wilderness if God performs enough miracles.

4. Meditate on the following statements dealing with your personal relationship with God.
   • If we don't have God internally, we always have to look for Him externally.
   • God works greatly through us when He dwells richly in us.

5. Using Deuteronomy 8:3,16 as references, list three reasons God performed the miracle of manna. Are these typical reasons people look for miracles?

   _____

   _____

   _____

   _____

   _____

6. How is God blessing you by not performing a miracle for every crisis in your life?

_____

_____

_____

_____

_____

_____

7. Pam received the answer to her prayer in a way that she did not anticipate or initially care for. Could God be answering your prayer in a similar fashion? Do you have an example of when God's manna ceased in your life and you had to make an adjustment that stressed you before it blessed you.

_____

_____

_____

_____

_____

_____

8. What, if any, revelation has God spoken to you from this unit?

_____

_____

_____

_____

_____

9. What action items can you develop to apply the concepts of this unit?
   Action Item #1:

   _____

   _____

   _____

   Action Item #2:

   _____

   _____

   _____

Unit Jewel:

If we don't have God internally, we always have to look for Him externally. God works greatly through us when He dwells richly in us.

Unit Summary:

Expect miracles, but don't expect them to fall from the Sky. Entering the Promised Land requires our partnering with God to see the miraculous happen and not just waiting on Him to perform miracles.

Meditation/Prayer Focus:

The Lord will send a blessing on your barns and on everything you put your hand to. The Lord your God will bless you in the land he is giving you.

—Deuteronomy 28:8

Lord, Manna is not your best for me. The manna has ceased so I can be increased. Through the manna I have been taught, humbled, and tested. Now, Lord, guide my steps. Lead me out of this wilderness and into the Promised Land of Your provision.

God's Payment Plan

Life Speaks: Brandon Hamilton

When Brandon was asked by the Elder board to consider making a pledge for the building fund, without hesitation he agreed. It wasn't as if it was an outrageous amount that was being asked of him and the way the payments were scheduled over a three-year period made Brandon feel comfortable with the pledge.

Lay-Away or ninety days same as cash?

Years ago, when credit wasn't extended as easily as it is today, there were lay-away plans. With lay-away a store reserves your merchandise while you make regular install-ment payments. Once you have made all the payments, you can take the merchandise home.

Today, in addition to lay-away, we have ninety days same as cash, no payments for six months, and all types of other payment options. These plans allow us to have our merchandise today and not pay for it until some time in the future. The evolution from lay-away payment plans to the various credit plans we have today, to a large extent, is based on trust.

When it comes to receiving material blessings, God can set us up on any kind of plan He wants. He can:

- Give blessings to us free
- Give blessings to us at a discount
- Make us lay them away or set us up on installments
- Not give them to us at all

When we have a personal relationship with God, it's easy to expect Him to give us everything free of charge, or expect God to bless us now on the promise we'll pay later. The only problem is that often the installments we promise are on hold until we can work through a situation.

Maybe we promised God that once a certain situation occurs, we would start tithing, teach Sunday school, or get involved in ministry in other ways. We must remember, however, that God is in charge of the goods, and He, not we, determines the payment plan. The world looks at credit history to develop a trust factor. God, however, does not penalize us based on the past. Instead He knows our future. Based on our character today, He knows if He can trust us to make those installments in the future.

When it comes to the things God has called us to do, sometimes we prefer a lay-away plan in which we don't take immediate ownership. But when it comes to the things we desire of God, we would rather have a plan that allows us to have what we want now and pay for it later. We're praying and waiting on God to deliver what we want and He's waiting on us to start making some faith installments on what He wants.

Life Speaks

Over a year had passed and Brandon had not made his first building pledge payment. It seemed every time he thought about giving, something else would always come up more pressing that would require the money; not to mention the motorcycle and the annual golf trip that now was quarterly. Brandon rationalized that the money for the things he wanted had regularly scheduled due dates whereas the church wouldn't need his money for at least a year or two.

God is waiting for us to put our materialistic dreams and goals on lay-away and not His agenda. He's waiting for us to realize that when we lay away our dreams, goals, and worldly desires and make a sizable deposit of our time and resources into the kingdom of God, we will be richly blessed.

The book of Haggai gives us a great lesson on God's payment plan. Remember, God can put us on any type of plan He wants. What plan He decides to put us on will depend on His grace, mercy, and purpose for our lives, along with our commitment to doing His will.

Don't lose interest!

[1] In the second year of King Darius, on the first day of the sixth month, the word of the LORD came through the prophet Haggai to Zerubbabel son of Shealtiel, governor of Judah, and to Joshua son of Jehozadak, the high priest: [2] This is what the LORD Almighty says: "These people say, 'The time has not yet come for the LORD's house to be built.' "

—Haggai 1:1,2

The church in Jerusalem was destroyed, and after work on the foundation had started, the people lost interest in the project. If we want God to give us a favorable payment plan for the things we want, we cannot put off the work of the kingdom. We cannot neglect what God is trying to accomplish.

Give it some thought.

[3] Then the word of the LORD came through the prophet Haggai: [4] "Is it a time for you yourselves to be living in your paneled houses, while this house remains a ruin?" [5] Now this is what the LORD Almighty says: "Give careful thought to your ways.

—Haggai 1:3-5

By Haggai's response we realize that these people weren't homeless. They just wanted nicer homes more than they wanted to serve God. Christians rarely admit that they are no longer concerned with the things of God. Our actions, however, show that personal endeavors have taken first priority in our lives. God told His people to consider their ways and is telling us the same thing. He wants us to take time to evaluate the quality and priority of our financial decisions because this will help determine what kind of payment plan He puts us on.

Life Speaks

After a job promotion, Brandon moved from his modest apartment into a very nice Condo. He made three consecutive monthly payments on his building pledge, but then he stopped and began to question the need for the new church building. Financially, Brandon had it all worked out on paper, but then unexpected bills began to come from everywhere. Once again Brandon found himself in the familiar situation of not having enough paycheck to cover the month.

Oh, you don't like this plan?

[6] You have planted much, but have harvested little. You eat, but never have enough. You drink, but never have your fill. You put on clothes, but are not warm. You earn wages, only to put them in a purse with holes in it." [7] This is what the LORD Almighty says: "Give careful thought to your ways.

—Haggai 1:6,7

Unfortunately this is a payment plan with which many of us are all too familiar. With this plan you work hard, but it never seems like there's enough money. We defined this earlier as Struggle Class. We think we need more money, but God says it's a matter of misplaced priorities. If we change our ways by reordering our priorities, God can change the payment plan that we're on. We don't have to stay in Struggle Class. God not only wants to meet our basic needs; He also wants to bless us with the desires of our heart. He has a much better plan for us if we are willing to examine our ways and put His agenda first.

Changing the payment plan

[8] Go up into the mountains and bring down timber and build the house, so that I may take pleasure in it and be honored," says the LORD.

—Haggai 1:8

It is so easy to say, "Okay, God, I've considered my ways and I promise I'm going to change! Now can you change my payment plan?" But God shows us that the way to change the payment plan is by building His church. This verse reminds us that we can become so obsessed with our pleasure that we forget that we are not the focus. God says build My church and I will take pleasure in it and I will be honored. Today, the call to support the church may be for a physical building or the programs of our church. Either way, the first order of business in God changing our payment plan is to understand that pleasing God should come before pleasing ourselves.

It doesn't matter what kind of adjustments we have to make in our lives or how difficult those changes may be. If God is not first in our lives, no type of payment plan is going to satisfy us. This is why even rich people can get depressed. Many of them are not satisfied with their plan because, even with all their money, life is not giving them the installments of joy, peace, and happiness that they expected.

God is responsible for the plan you're on.

9 "You expected much, but see, it turned out to be little. What you brought home, I blew away. Why?" declares the LORD Almighty. "Because of my house, which remains a ruin, while each of you is busy with his own house. 10 Therefore, because of you the heavens have withheld their dew and the earth its crops. 11 I called for a drought on the fields and the mountains, on the grain, the new wine, the oil and whatever the ground produces, on men and cattle, and on the labor of your hands."

—Haggai 1:9-11

There is always someone else on whom to place the blame when we are in Struggle Class and are not happy with our payment plan. We can accuse our spouse, our job, the devil, or countless others. God reminds us that there is no need to look for fault in others because He takes full responsibility. God intentionally wrecks our resources when we neglect His church. The change in the payment plan that can turn our financial lives around starts with our focus on God's church.

I am with you.

12 Then Zerubbabel son of Shealtiel, Joshua son of Jehozadak, the high priest, and the whole remnant of the people obeyed the voice of the LORD their God and the message

of the prophet Haggai, because the LORD their God had sent him. And the people feared the LORD. [13] Then Haggai, the LORD's messenger, gave this message of the LORD to the people: "I am with you," declares the LORD. [14] So the LORD stirred up the spirit of Zerubbabel son of Shealtiel, governor of Judah, and the spirit of Joshua son of Jehozadak, the high priest, and the spirit of the whole remnant of the people. They came and began to work on the house of the LORD Almighty, their God, [15] on the twenty-fourth day of the sixth month in the second year of King Darius.

—Haggai 1:12-15

In verse 1 Haggai spoke to the people in the first day of the sixth month. But it wasn't until the 24th day of the sixth month before the people really changed. We can tell God we're sorry and that we want to change the payment plan we're on, but how much time goes by before we actually begin to do what we're supposed to do? Nevertheless, it is comforting to know, as verse 13 indicates, that despite our shortcomings, God is still with us!

Ninety days same as a blessing?

[15] " 'Now give careful thought to this from this day on—consider how things were before one stone was laid on another in the LORD's temple. [16] When anyone came to a heap of twenty measures, there were only ten. When anyone went to a wine vat to draw fifty measures, there were only twenty. [17] I struck all the work of your hands with blight, mildew and hail, yet you did not turn to me,' declares the LORD. [18] 'From this day on, from this twenty-fourth day of the ninth month, give careful thought to the day when the foundation of the LORD's temple was laid. Give careful thought.

—Haggai 2:15-18

God wanted to remind the Israelites how it used to be before they recommitted to working on the church. He wanted them to remember what kind of payment plan they were on and the trials that came their way. He wanted them to remember times they thought they had a $20 bill in their wallet and only found a $10 bill. Then in verse 18 God told them to remember from this day forward. The day was the 24th day of the ninth month. That was three months or roughly ninety days after they started working. It was approximately ninety days of working on God's church before God told them that good things would start happening for them.

They didn't get their blessing first and then pay for it in ninety days. They had to first build up the kingdom of God and then in approximately ninety days God changed their payment plan. God didn't offer this plan to them up front and we shouldn't view it as a formula. The point is, God often wants to see the dedication and consistency of our commitment over time before He changes the payment plan we're on. He wants to see if we will let life's situations cause us to lose interest in the things of God again.

[19] Is there yet any seed left in the barn? Until now, the vine and the fig tree, the pomegranate and the olive tree have not borne fruit. " 'From this day on I will bless you.' "

—Haggai 2:19

God reminded them that during the ninety days of working on the church, nothing had changed in their lives. They had gone through and passed a time of testing and then God informed them that the payment plan would change and the blessings would begin.

We do not know what type of payment plan God will put us on. But we can be sure that there is a correlation between what we invest in the things of God and the payment plan we are on.

Life Speaks

Brandon was furious! How dare the elder board contact him about his pledge. So what if it had been a year since his last payment. What he had contributed in three payments was probably more than many people had given. What was it with those church people—always asking for more money. Where does it really go anyway? Brandon was resolved. It was time to give the whole church scene a nice long break.

Whether it's a bill from a creditor or from God, too often our mindset is, how can I skip a payment? How can I get out of this commitment and maybe pay it later. How can I get out of this so I can do what I want? With this attitude we are only cheating and disqualifying ourselves from receiving God's best payment plan, which is to bless us beyond our needs for the purpose of promoting His kingdom.

When we refuse to honor God we are choosing to work for manna. Would you accept a job at an agreed salary and be content if your paycheck was regularly much smaller than expected? Relying on manna is like working for far less than you have been promised. This is why we need to be on God's best payment plan.

Unit Review

1. If we want God to give us a favorable payment plan we cannot _____ the work of the kingdom.

2. According to Haggai 1:9-11 who or what determines if we are placed on a bad payment plan?

   ____ Satan

   ____ Ourselves

   ____ God

   ____ Bad luck

3. What are the consequences of skipping payments without permission? What might be the consequences of skipping spiritual payments to God?

   _____

   _____

   _____

4. Check the correct statement.

   ____ If I faithfully serve God for ninety days, then He will bless me with what I want.

   ____ God often wants to see my consistency and dedication over time before He changes my payment plan.

5. What assignments has God given to you that you still have in lay-away? Why is it to your advantage to make completing these assignments a priority?

   _____

   _____

   _____

6. God asked the people numerous times to consider their ways. Will you commit to a time of meditation and dedicated prayer this week for this purpose of considering your ways and your financial situation?

   Date: _____ What were your conclusions?_____

   _____

   _____

   _____

   _____

   _____

7. After being out of church for six months Brandon eventually joined another church that was larger, newer, and would be less likely to bother him about money. Do you think his payment plan got better with his new beginning? Explain.

   _____

   _____

   _____

   _____

   _____

8. What, if any, revelation has God spoken to you from this unit?

   _____

   _____

   _____

   _____

   _____

9. What action items can you develop to apply the concepts of this unit?

Action Item #1:

_____

_____

_____

_____

Action Item #2:

_____

_____

_____

_____

Unit Jewel:

God is waiting for us to put our materialistic dreams and goals on lay away and not His agenda.

Unit Summary:

Our dedication to the work of the kingdom is a key factor in determining what kind of payment plan God puts us on.

Meditation/Prayer Focus:

For I know the plans I have for you, declares the Lord, plans to give you hope and a future.

—Jeremiah 29:11

Though I am unable to see it now, Lord, help me to trust that you have a plan for my life that is better than what I'm currently experiencing.

Give and It Shall Be Given

Life speaks: Michelle Babcock

The last thing Michelle had planned for her life was becoming a single mom. She didn't want the divorce, but after just two short years of marriage, Dexter decided that he wasn't ready for commitment.

Giving is a matter of trust

[38] Give, and it will be given to you. A good measure, pressed down, shaken together and running over, will be poured into your lap. For with the measure you use, it will be measured to you."

—Luke 6:38

How can giving get us what we want? More than money, this is an issue of trust. We give to those we trust and feel comfortable with. Sadly, we often trust the world, which can give us no guarantees, more than we trust God, Who can never fail.

In the world we trust in dreams, employers, education, the government, the legal system, friends, and family, all of which can and have failed us. That's the way of the world. Yet no matter how much we are disappointed, we keep on giving to and trusting in the system believing if we give enough, something will be given back to us. We give ourselves to work dead-end jobs. We give in to unhealthy relationships that obviously are not working. We give because we have hope that things will change.

Life Speaks

How Michelle loved, depended on, and trusted Dexter. The signs of his immaturity, however, were there before the marriage, but Michelle chose to ignore them. She hoped that married life would bring about the much-needed maturity in Dexter. But it never happened, and now Dexter was no longer there. Though it wouldn't be easy, Michelle realized she had to move on.

We can be very diligent applying the biblical principle of giving to realize our personal pursuits, but we sometimes have a problem applying it to our spiritual pursuits. Can the world do no wrong? Is God stretching one hand out saying, "Give and it shall be given" with the other hand behind His back and its fingers crossed? The world can show us both hands and still lie to our face, yet we keep on giving into the system. Should we not be able to trust God who gives us the very breath of life?

When we fail to trust God, we will entrust and invest more into our dreams than we do into the kingdom of God. We will end up with a powerless, resented religion instead of powerful, life-changing Christianity. When people see us truly living for and giving to the kingdom, there will be fewer skeptics and a lot more converts. But it all starts with what we are willing to give and who we are willing to trust.

Life Speaks

If what she was dealing with was not enough, Michelle also felt guilty for not being able to continue tithing to her church. She was grateful that the church was supportive and understanding, but out of her love for God she insisted on giving something every time she received income.

The motive for giving

The worldly motive for giving is often to get something in return. In Christianity, the motive for giving is love. The world cannot promise that you will receive something in return, but the Bible does. When we give because of love, God gives back to us. Love is the motive; receiving is a by-product. Giving just to receive may get us the desired results, but it cannot compare to the results that could be received when we give out of love. Neither does giving to receive promote the unity of the Spirit that is so desperately needed in the church.

[20] You may charge a foreigner interest, but not a brother Israelite, so that the LORD your God may bless you in everything you put your hand to in the land you are entering to possess.

—Deuteronomy 23:20

If someone asked you for a loan you could charge them interest if you wanted. But when you are dealing with God's people, making a profit should not be your primary concern, especially if they are in need. The primary motive is to advance love and unity. When this is your focus, God begins to bless you and the work you do.

The pain of today vs the pain of delay

When children get splinters in their fingers, they may hesitate to give their hands to their parents. If they give, however, then healing will be given unto them. Likewise, as adults dealing with our heavenly Father, there is still that element of fear and distrust. We know that God has what's best, but we know it might be painful. If we are ever going to get to where God can best use us, we must understand that the pain of delay is usually greater than the pain of today.

That splinter may hurt today, but if we keep delaying, the finger will get infected. If we spend our lives always trying to figure out how to get more, if we never give our hand to God to remove the splinter, things in our lives can become infected with sin and worldliness. This infection can greatly reduce our chances of receiving.

> ## Life Speaks
>
> "I don't know how long I can do this!" Michele would cry out to God. But it wouldn't be ten seconds later that she would burst out into laughter. Many times she had made the decision to forego items she needed so she could maintain her faithfulness to giving something to the church. It always tore at her, but she knew what was in her heart to do.
>
> Each time she gave, however, God always sent an angel. There was an anonymous money order in the mail with the words, "God loves you" in the notes section. A lady in church had received seven boxes of diapers from a baby shower, but she decided to use cloth diapers and gave the boxes to Michelle. The deacons' wives got together and brought enough food and baby items to last a month or more. God was truly blessing her and meeting her needs. Michelle cried when she thought she couldn't do it alone. She laughed when she realized she didn't have to.

The very joy we seek in life, that the world tells us comes from getting, actually comes by giving to God. The world offers us temporary joy that appears painless. But one day the honeymoon will be over and we'll have to work at the marriage. At some point the newness will wear off the car or the house and the reality of maintenance will set in. Eventually we may find ourselves at the top of the corporate ladder, yet wondering why we don't feel complete.

God offers us everlasting joy, which is our strength. It is not dependent on what we do or do not possess. Instead, it is based on trusting and giving ourselves to Him and enduring the pain of godly discipline today, which in the long run is far less painful than if we choose to delay.

What is your staff?

Is there something in your life that you won't give to God? Is there a cherished security blanket that you are holding on to? Psalms 84:11 says, "**No good thing does he withhold from those whose walk is blameless.**" If you are holding on to something worthwhile and you give it to God, He may bless it for greater service and give it back to you. Why?

Because by being willing to give it up, you are submitting to God's Lordship. You are showing that your trust is not in the thing you were clinging to, but in Him. Moses and his staff are a good example of this.

> [1] Now Moses was tending the flock of Jethro his father-in-law, the priest of Midian, and he led the flock to the far side of the desert and came to Horeb, the mountain of God.
>
> —Exodus 3:1

Moses was a shepherd and depended on his staff for protection for him and his sheep. But God had a new assignment for Moses. In the same way that Jesus told the disciples that they would become fishers of men, God would tell Moses that he was going to herd God's people and lead them out of Egypt into the Promised Land.

> [1] Moses answered, "What if they do not believe me or listen to me and say, 'The LORD did not appear to you'"?
>
> —Exodus 4:1

Picture Moses standing before God, gripping his staff ever so firmly. He was very uncomfortable with this new assignment and was holding on to one thing in his life that made him feel secure from day to day—his staff.

> [2] Then the LORD said to him, "What is that in your hand?" "A staff," he replied.
>
> —Exodus 4:2

God knew what was in Moses' hand, but He was revealing to Moses something that was in his spiritual blind spot. It was as if God were saying, "Of course you're doubtful, look at what you are holding on to and trusting in instead of Me."

Throw it down!

> [3] The LORD said, "Throw it on the ground." Moses threw it on the ground and it became a snake, and he ran from it.
>
> —Exodus 4:3

The staff represented worldly protection. Casting it down, therefore, showed openness and vulnerability. Likewise, we need to give up those things we think are protecting us and learn to depend on God. The police tell the thief to throw down his gun, but he starts shooting. He feels like he has nothing to depend on but his gun. So he holds it and it ends up costing him his life. Dropping what you think is protecting you takes faith. It takes realizing that if you want to live, you need to place your trust in something or someone more reliable.

What's in your spiritual blind spot that you trust and won't give to God? What are you holding on to as if your life depended on it? Pray and ask God to reveal it to you so you can throw it down.

Moses knew he was holding a good thing, but as he gave up the staff, God revealed to him how dangerous it was to trust in it. How many times have we been bitten by the very thing we put so much trust in? When the "good" thing keeps biting us, it's time to reassess our relationship with it. We must learn that until we give up our staff, we won't believe that it's harming us.

Moses couldn't see this until he surrendered the staff to God and the same holds true for us. What is your staff today? Is it your job, spouse, bank account, possessions, children, a dream, or an addiction? Whatever it is, know for a fact that only God can be depended on to never fail you. When we refuse to surrender the negative to God, we restrict the positive that He wants to give us. When we refuse to lessen our dependency on the good, we restrict God from enhancing it or blessing us with better.

Life Speaks

Dexter was the best thing that ever happened to Michelle, so she thought at first. There were numerous occasions where she was hurt by Dexter, many times where she was tempted to give up on the marriage. But she held on to the relationship. Even though Dexter was the one who left, God showed Michelle that she had some releasing and reevaluating to do.

Picking up the empowered staff

[4] Then the LORD said to him, "Reach out your hand and take it by the tail." So Moses reached out and took hold of the snake and it turned back into a staff in his hand. [5] "This," said the LORD, "is so that they may believe that the LORD, the God of their fathers—the God of Abraham, the God of Isaac and the God of Jacob—has appeared to you."

—Exodus 4:4,5

Moses got his staff back because he entrusted it to God. When we give something to God, if its purpose has not been fulfilled in our lives God will give it back. God simply wants to take the good things we give Him and anoint them for a greater witness and service. The staff that we have stewardship over is not just for us; it is to be used for the glory of God. If and when we understand this, we will have a whole new perspective on giving to God. It will be much easier to resign our resources to God because we know He will bless and return them to us. Give and it shall be given to you. Give out of love, knowing that it underpins the kingdom and God gives an excellent return on investments.

By giving, Moses got a blessing that he was not expecting. In Exodus 4:2 all Moses had was a staff, but in Exodus 4:20 after Moses gave the staff up and got it back, it was referred to as the staff of God. This instrument, that at one time was only used for shepherding, now had a multitude of purposes. Moses hit the water of the Nile with it and the river turned to blood. Moses stretched it over the waters and caused frogs to come up on the land. Moses struck the ground with it and the dust became lice. Moses lifted it toward heaven and thunder, hail, and fire ran along the ground.

When you give something valuable to God, the possibilities are endless as to how powerful it will be when He returns it to you. Do you want your life to be supernaturally energized by God? Do you want your job, finances, and relationships to be empowered by God? Whatever it is that you want God to bless, you have to give it to Him first. It's not just a matter of giving God control. It also involves God, at some point, giving control back to you.

When do you get control back? You get it the same time Moses got it back. The answer is in Exodus 4:4. You get control back when you take God at his word and are ready to grab the snake by the tail. You get custody when you are ready to trust God to help you take charge over the thing that has been controlling you.

Life Speaks

Dexter would often call trying to manipulate Michelle. Initially she complied because she thought he would come back. She soon found that once again, Dexter was only thinking of himself. When she grew tired of the games and the excuses and realized that her trust needed to be in God, God began to empower Michelle's life. He gave her the strength to let Dexter know in no uncertain terms the requirements he would have to meet before she would even consider reconciliation.

When Moses gave up his staff to God and saw it for what it really was, he fled. There are some things in life that we run to that we should be running from. What is your staff today? Who or what are you running to and depending on more than God? God is saying, "Throw it down."

We may say that giving to God is hard, and sometimes it is. But we have to also consider how we often give in to the world system without hesitation. It's all a matter of trust, because we give more readily to those whom we trust. If we say that we love God, we must learn to trust Him. "Give and it shall be given unto you" can also be stated, "Trust and it shall be entrusted unto you."

Life Speaks

With newfound faith, strength and confidence, Michelle applied for and got a job paying her twice as much as her previous position. The job also allowed her to work from home so she could be with her daughter. Michelle was far from being over the divorce, but she was well on her way to recovery. Even when she felt she had so little to give, she gave, and much was given back to her.

Manna represents a one-way flow and we're always on the receiving end. As we grow accustomed to not reciprocating, we feel as though receiving is an entitlement. The very thought of giving then seems foreign to us; and if we do give, it is with much pause and anguish.

Remember, how much we give to God, whether it be money, time, talent, hopes, or dreams, is a direct indication of how much we trust Him. It is a direct indication of how powerful we will be as Christians. Give and it shall be given.

Unit Review

1. If giving is a matter of trust, whom does your giving reflect that you are trusting in?

   _____

   _____

   _____

   _____

   _____

   _____

2. T/F ____ Love is the motive for giving in Christianity.

   T/F ____ The world promises and always delivers a return on your giving.

   T/F ____ Giving with any motive promotes the unity of the Spirit needed in the church.

   T/F ____ The pain of delay is usually greater than the pain of today.

3. Like Moses, often we are reluctant to surrender things to God. What can Psalms 84:11 teach us to help in this area?

   _____

   _____

   _____

   _____

   _____

   _____

4. Check the correct statements.

    ___ We should never give up things we need.

    ___ Giving up things we depend on shows an openness and vulnerability to the will of God.

    ___ Sometimes the thing we hold on to is what keeps us from a life empowered by God.

    ___ Giving up things we depend on often helps us to see that thing in a different light.

5. What is your staff? What do you trust and depend on more than God? Has it ever bitten you?

_____

_____

_____

_____

6. Although it may be common to reduce or stop giving to God when things get tight, Michelle continued to be faithful when she had little to give. Why does God delight to honor that type of sacrificial giving?

_____

_____

_____

7. What, if any, revelation has God spoken to you from this unit?

_____

_____

_____

8. What action items can you develop to apply the concepts of this unit?
   Action Item #1:

   _____

   _____

   _____

   Action Item #2:

   _____

   _____

   _____

Unit Jewel:

When you give something valuable to God, the possibilities are endless as to how powerful it will be when He returns it to you.

Unit Summary:

Giving is a matter of trust. When we are willing to trust God with what is legitimately important to us, He will empower it for greater service.

Meditation/Prayer Focus:

God is not a man, that he should lie, nor a son of man, that he should change his mind. Does he speak and then not act? Does he promise and not fulfill?

—Numbers 23:19

Lord, your Word says give and it shall be given. I trust You, Lord. You are not a liar. Teach me how to become a giver. Show me how to release what I hold to so tightly that I may embrace You and the fullness of Your provision.

Getting to Your Blessing

Life Speaks: Jonathan Lee

Nate was the oldest and dad's favorite. He was a naturally gifted athlete with looks and a great personality. It didn't take long before my admiration of my brother turned to envy and then hatred. Competing against him was useless, but you better believe I tried!

But one Sunday in church the pastor preached a sermon on "Finding your niche in life." For some reason, that day I happened to be listening, really listening. It was as if the sermon had my name, Jonathan H. Lee, written all over it. I left church that day resolved to cultivate the "nerd gene" that had been passed down to me. I went on to become a successful architect and now have my own firm.

It took awhile, but one day I worked up the nerve to call Nate and apologize to him. He didn't have a clue what I was talking about, but that's OK. I did what I felt God was leading me to do. I now realize that I had to get over "Nate the Great" in order to get to where God wanted me to be.

Getting past the perception of limited resources

We all want to be blessed in some way, but there is a right way to go about it. The wrong way looks quicker and easier and that's why many people take it. But experience, painfully and repeatedly, teaches us that going about things the wrong way turns blessings into curses. We're born with a desire to be blessed immediately. The baby's cry, the toddler's tantrum, the child's whining, and the teenager's rebellion—unfortunately, we often continue in these ways even as adults.

The Bible tells the story of Rebekah who was pregnant with twins who struggled within her womb. Esau was born first but Jacob came out holding onto Esau's heel. That scenario sums up our attitude toward blessings. We want to be first and we can't stand to see people getting ahead of us. We're driven by the fear of limited resources running out, rather than having faith to believe that God has unlimited resources. Therefore, we often perceive blessings are getting away from us and going to others.

Jacob was sold on the concept of limited blessings. As the younger son, Jacob was not entitled to as much of an inheritance as Esau. After a hunting trip, Esau returned home famished. Esau was then talked into selling his birthright to Jacob for a bowl of stew. Then Jacob plotted with his mother to obtain the family blessing from his father that rightfully belonged to his older brother Esau. The following verses record Esau's response after finding out Jacob had tricked him.

[36] Esau said, "Isn't he rightly named Jacob? He has deceived me these two times: He took my birthright, and now he's taken my blessing!" Then he asked, "Haven't you reserved any blessing for me?" [37] Isaac answered Esau, "I have made him lord over you and have made all his relatives his servants, and I have sustained him with grain and new wine. So what can I possibly do for you, my son?" [38] Esau said to his father, "Do you have only one blessing, my father? Bless me too, my father!" Then Esau wept aloud. [39] His father Isaac answered him, "Your dwelling will be away from the earth's richness, away from the dew of heaven above. [40] You will live by the sword and you will serve your brother. But when you grow restless, you will throw his yoke from off your neck." [41] Esau held a grudge against Jacob because of the blessing his father had given him. He said to himself, "The days of mourning for my father are near; then I will kill my brother Jacob." [42] When Rebekah was told what her older son Esau had said, she sent for her younger son Jacob and said to him, "Your brother Esau is consoling himself with the thought of killing you. [43] Now then, my son, do what I say: Flee at once to my brother Laban in Haran.

—Genesis 27:36-43

Was Jacob really blessed if he always had to look over his shoulder wondering when his brother would come to kill him? How blessed are we if we can never settle down and enjoy our blessing? If you see your blessing turning into a curse, you need to reexamine how you got it. When people are sold on the concept of limited blessings, they press to be blessed, but before long they're trying to disperse the curse.

> ### Life Speaks
>
> If not for that sermon from Pastor Steve, I might not be enjoying my life today. I didn't have a life. My whole existence revolved around being a pain to Nate. I was angry and bitter and there was no limit to the ways I was going to make Nate's life miserable. The fact is, I couldn't see what God wanted to do with me because I only saw the blessings being limited to Nate's life. I was the one who was miserable.

Getting to where God wants you to be

Jacob went to live with his uncle Laban, but his sinister ways had not changed. In the following verses he was accused of cheating Laban.

> [1] Jacob heard that Laban's sons were saying, "Jacob has taken everything our father owned and has gained all this wealth from what belonged to our father." [2] And Jacob noticed that Laban's attitude toward him was not what it had been. [3] Then the LORD said to Jacob, "Go back to the land of your fathers and to your relatives, and I will be with you."
>
> —Genesis 31:1-3

One of the first steps of getting to our blessing is realizing that we need to be where God wants us. Sometimes, because we got our blessing our way, we are far from where God wants us. This could be geographically, in our finances, employment, relationships, body, mind, or spiritual life. Jacob's scheming caused him to have to leave home and also got him in trouble with his father-in-law. God told Jacob to go back home, but when Jacob left, Laban tracked him down. At first everything was fine between Laban and Jacob. They were cheating each other and both were happy. But Jacob's blessings started to exceed Laban's blessing and Laban didn't like that.

When you're trying to get your blessings by ungodly means, you'll find that the people you have affiliated with won't take too kindly when they see you prospering more than they. This is why Laban came after Jacob. People in the world don't want to see you come back home to God if your return impacts them. They will do everything they can to keep you in the world. Getting to your blessing means getting to where God would have you to be and understanding that other people are not always going to be happy about your leaving them behind.

Getting to your blessing without injuring others

[1] Jacob also went on his way, and the angels of God met him. [2] When Jacob saw them, he said, "This is the camp of God!" So he named that place Mahanaim. [3] Jacob sent messengers ahead of him to his brother Esau in the land of Seir, the country of Edom. [4] He instructed them: "This is what you are to say to my master Esau: 'Your servant Jacob says, I have been staying with Laban and have remained there till now. [5] I have cattle and donkeys, sheep and goats, menservants and maidservants. Now I am sending this message to my lord, that I may find favor in your eyes.' " [6] When the messengers returned to Jacob, they said, "We went to your brother Esau, and now he is coming to meet you, and four hundred men are with him." [7] In great fear and distress Jacob divided the people who were with him into two groups, and the flocks and herds and camels as well.

—Genesis 32:1-7

Romans 12:18 says, "If it is possible, as far as it depends on you, live at peace with everyone." We have to get our blessings in ways that don't harm others. Jacob was trying to obey God by returning home, but because of his past indiscretions, he was worried about his brother killing him. Jacob then came up with another plan of trying to buy favor from his brother by sending him gifts. Never underestimate the impact that people in your past can have on your future. Jacob was not free to do what God had called him to do because of something he had done long ago.

Our past actions don't necessarily make getting to our blessings impossible, but they surely can make them harder to obtain. What we do in the present will one day be in our past, but still can impact our future. The blessings we want in the future all start with how we treat people today.

Life Speaks

I had always made straight A's in school. The first semester of my junior year in high school I struggled to get B's and C's. As the semester progressed I knew I wasn't doing too well, but at the time it didn't matter. I was a man possessed in my efforts to destroy Nate. When my report card came in the mail that Monday, it was a very sobering wake-up call. I was allowing my disdain for Nate to rob me of my future! This had to stop.

Nate was my brother. He had never done anything to me, and it was time that I gave him the respect he deserved. I wasn't going to worship him like everybody else, but neither could I allow him to continue to be my focus.

Getting over your own hurdles

Jacob had placed himself in quite a predicament and was faced with the consequences of his actions.

[11] Save me, I pray, from the hand of my brother Esau, for I am afraid he will come and attack me, and also the mothers with their children. [12] But you have said, 'I will surely make you prosper and will make your descendants like the sand of the sea, which cannot be counted.' "

—Genesis 32:11,12

God wanted to bless Jacob, but his brother wanted to kill him. Getting to your blessing may require you to get over hurdles you have placed in your own way. You may not think you can get over them and the question becomes, do you trust God or do you continue to trust in the things that got you into trouble in the first place? It's hard to change the way you do things, especially if you have been doing them for years. Jacob continued with his plan to buy his brother's favor. Same old Jacob—he wanted God's best, but couldn't let go of his old ways.

Getting over your wrestling moves

24 So Jacob was left alone, and a man wrestled with him till daybreak. 25 When the man saw that he could not overpower him, he touched the socket of Jacob's hip so that his hip was wrenched as he wrestled with the man. 26 Then the man said, "Let me go, for it is daybreak." But Jacob replied, "I will not let you go unless you bless me." 27 The man asked him, "What is your name?" "Jacob," he answered. 28 Then the man said, "Your name will no longer be Jacob, but Israel, because you have struggled with God and with men and have overcome." 29 Jacob said, "Please tell me your name." But he replied, "Why do you ask my name?" Then he blessed him there.

—Genesis 32:24-29

Jacob wrestling with the angel is symbolic of the intensity and tenacity we should have in our prayer lives. When we're trying to get to a blessing and problems are in our way, we don't need to plot, scheme, and wrestle with them. We need to spend serious time in prayer. Ephesians 6:10-13 reminds us that we don't get to our blessings by wrestling. The strength for getting to our blessings comes from the power of God and not solely from our ability to work out a good plan.

Jacob wanted to set things right with his brother, which is good. But we can mend relationships with people and still not get to our blessing. Sometimes it's not until we correct things with God that we get the victory. Getting to our blessing requires us to take our eyes off of people, situations, and circumstances and focus them directly on God through prayer.

The word "fight" is used throughout the Bible but all the references to people actually "wrestling" involved Jacob and his family. Jacob wrestled with the angel. Jacob's wife, Rachel spoke of how she wrestled with her sister Leah competing with her for the affection of Jacob. Rachel didn't understand that Leah wasn't her problem. Wrestling with flesh and blood means that we get locked up with the actions of people, and we continually let those actions bother us. Our attitude toward those we are wrestling with sours and we begin to plot.

Have you ever noticed that boxers throw punches and then back up to reassess the situation? When boxers stop fighting and start wrestling, the referee separates them. Every three minutes boxers retreat from the battle. They go and sit down, take a rest, receive counsel, get refreshed with water, and then they go back out to fight. That's how they fight a good fight. They don't hold on to each other's heels. Fighters only wrestle when they are tired or outmatched.

The devil is no match for the God in us, so when we start wrestling, that means we have not adequately prepared for the battle. We often go running out into life's battles unprepared, and in the first round instead of fighting, we're holding on, wrestling for dear life. What was meant to be a good fight with us coming out the winner turns into a wrestling match and we're the one with dirt on our back. We're good at wrestling, trying to take down a situation, but if we want our blessing, we have to wrestle in prayer, then get up and fight by faith.

Why was Jacob wrestling so hard with this angel? Why wouldn't he let go when the bell rang? Remember, Jacob had already formulated a plan. Now he wanted God to bless it. Sometimes we have the situation all figured out and we get serious in prayer wanting God to make it happen just the way we planned it. Sometimes God can't get through to us that He's not going to resolve the problem the way we've planned. But we won't let go. We keep pestering God to do what we want done.

We can become so set in our ways that often the only way God can get our attention is to allow us to get hurt. Something that was perfectly healthy in our life often has to become lame before we really listen to God instead of insisting that He listen to us.

Even after Jacob was injured, he still didn't give in. If we don't allow God to break our hold on our way of doing things, He may have to break us. The body of Christ is battered with an assortment of ailments. God wants to know if we've had enough yet. He wants to know if we are ready to let Him heal us so we can stop wrestling with flesh and blood and start fighting the good fight of faith.

The blessing that Jacob received was not God blessing his plan, but God changing his name. The name change was symbolic of a change in thinking. Jacob, now called Israel, was to no longer approach problems in his life in the same way that got him into past trouble. He began to think like a child of God with a future instead of a hustler on the run.

Getting to "I have enough"

⁴ But Esau ran to meet Jacob and embraced him; he threw his arms around his neck and kissed him. And they wept. ⁵ Then Esau looked up and saw the women and children. "Who are these with you?" he asked. Jacob answered, "They are the children God has

graciously given your servant." ⁶ Then the maidservants and their children approached and bowed down. ⁷ Next, Leah and her children came and bowed down. Last of all came Joseph and Rachel, and they too bowed down. ⁸ Esau asked, "What do you mean by all these droves I met?" "To find favor in your eyes, my lord," he said. ⁹ But Esau said, "I already have plenty, my brother. Keep what you have for yourself." ¹⁰ "No, please!" said Jacob. "If I have found favor in your eyes, accept this gift from me. For to see your face is like seeing the face of God, now that you have received me favorably.

—Genesis 33:4-10

Jacob's plan was to buy his brother's love, but Esau wasn't interested. We don't know what happened to Esau after Jacob left home, but God had already done a work in Esau's life before Jacob's plan even materialized. When Esau told Jacob that he had plenty, he was making the statement that life is not just about accumulating more stuff. Getting to your blessing is often a matter of being able to say you have enough and being truly at peace at the level of your material possessions.

¹If you will listen diligently to the voice of the Lord your God, being watchful to do all His commandments which I command you this day, the Lord your God will set you high above all the nations of the earth. ²And all these blessings shall come upon you and overtake you if you heed the voice of the Lord your God.

—Deuteronomy 28:1,2 (AMP)

As long as we listen to the voice of "Never enough," we never will have enough. But when God sees that we are focused on Him, we will find blessings overtaking us. We won't have to worry about getting to our blessings; they will start coming to us.

Getting to "I've had enough!"

Not only do you have to tell yourself, "I have enough;" you also have to tell yourself, "I have had enough." Esau had to tell himself, "I've had enough of being mad at my brother for what he did to me and dreaming how I can get him back. I've had enough of bitterness, hatred, and unforgiveness." When Esau got to this point, that's when he got to his real blessing. We cannot truly enjoy and appreciate our blessings until we have had enough of letting our flesh rule us. We will not be victorious if we insist on wrestling with how we were hurt, how unfair past circumstances were, and how much we had to suffer. As legitimate and painful as those feelings are, at some point we have to say, "I've had enough" and release them to God.

> [9]Do not repay evil with evil or insult with insult, but with blessing, because to this you were called so that you may inherit a blessing.
>
> —1 Peter 3:9

This verse reminds us that we are called to inherit a blessing. That inheritance is based on whether we tell ourselves that we have enough and we have had enough. This gives us the freedom to bless other people even when they deserve to be cursed. This gives us the freedom to trust God and lean not to our own understanding. This is imperative if we are to get to our blessing.

Many people have wanted something in life and when they obtained it, it wasn't what they thought it would be. The question is, do we really know what our blessing is? Getting to our blessing is not so much obtaining a goal we have set for ourselves; it's getting to God's perfect will for our lives.

Life Speaks

I can see it so clearly now. At the time I really didn't know what I wanted in life. It was Nate's goal to be the starting quarterback on the team. It was my goal to make the team to steal some of the glory from him. But in all honesty I didn't even want to play football. I now realize that God had a plan for my life all along that had absolutely nothing to do with Nate.

Jesus, speaking to the crowd in John 6:49, said, "Your forefathers ate the manna in the desert, yet they died." What is the point of getting to your blessing if it brings some form of death into your life? The message of this Scripture is that the time for manna has passed. There is so much more to life than the accumulation of manna. There are so many greater blessings that we should be pursuing.

Unit Review

1. What are some of the dangers of buying into the concept of limited resources?

    _____

    _____

    _____

    _____

2. Getting to your blessing means getting to where God wants you to be. Circle the areas where you feel you are not where God would have you to be. What is your plan for getting there?

Spiritual life	Geographic location	Finances
Health	Relationships	Career
Education	Other _____	

3. The _____ that we want in the future all start with how we _____ people today.

4. Explain how getting to your blessing also takes getting to reconciliation.

    _____

    _____

    _____

    _____

5. Explain the concepts of getting to "I have enough" and "I've had enough."

    _____

    _____

    _____

6. What does 1 Peter 3:9 call on us to do that we might inherit our blessing?

    _____

    _____

    _____

7. Jonathan, just like Jacob, felt that his brother stood in the way of his receiving God's blessing. Is the rivalry between siblings any more or less intense than that of co-workers when there is the perception of limited blessings?

    _____

    _____

    _____

8. What, if any, revelation has God spoken to you from this unit?

    _____

    _____

    _____

9. What action items can you develop to apply the concepts of this unit?
    Action Item #1:

    _____

    _____

    _____

    Action Item #2:

    _____

    _____

    _____

Unit Jewel:

Things we do in the present will one day be in our past, but still can impact our future. The blessings we want in the future all start with how we treat people today.

Unit Summary:

The end does not justify the means in getting to our blessing. There is no shortage with God, so it is imperative that we not mistreat others as we attempt to get our blessing.

Meditation/Prayer Focus:

A faithful man will be richly blessed, but one eager to get rich will not go unpunished.
—Proverbs 28:20

Lord, replace my eagerness with faithfulness.

Working Your Blessing

Life Speaks: Bryan Higgins

Me? A workaholic? Not really. I know how to relax, unwind, and spend quality time with family and friends. It's just that as much as I enjoy things like football, golf, and television, I can't justify spending every free moment I have pursuing them. Time is the one commodity that I cannot get back and I want to spend it wisely to ensure that I leave behind a true Christian legacy.

I enjoy my job, but I'm not content to work 9 to 5 until I retire. God has blessed me with creativity and an entrepreneurial spirit that beckons me to do better for myself and elevate God's kingdom. I'm not a workaholic. I'm just working my blessing!

Producers work their blessing

[15] The LORD God took the man and put him in the Garden of Eden to work it and take care of it. [16] And the LORD God commanded the man, "You are free to eat from any tree in the garden;

—Genesis 2:15,16

What do you do in a garden full of the best fruit in the world? You eat! God told Adam and Eve they could freely eat of all of the trees of the garden except one. They were, however, given the direction to maintain the garden before they were told to eat of it. The biggest problem with blessings is not that they are so few, but that we are consumption oriented.

When we put consumption before maintenance, the blessing is not going to last very long. We have to find and cultivate ways to make our blessings grow. We have to identify and weed out things that cause them to die.

God has called us to be stewards over everything. As stewards we must develop the mindset of a producer and not just a consumer. Thinking like a producer requires hard work. But as a consumer it's easy to know what to do with money. You get it and you spend it! With that mentality, we honestly believe that the answer to our problem is always more money or blessings. The reality is sometimes we have an income problem, but more often than we want to admit, we have a stewardship problem.

Stewardship requires putting aside living for the moment so that our blessings can be extended into the future and for the kingdom. A selfish consumption-oriented steward brings pain and suffering to self and others where God intended blessings. For example, in Genesis 3:6 Eve contemplated all the ways that she and Adam could be blessed by the forbidden fruit. Against the counsel of God, Adam and Eve ate of the tree of knowledge. Likewise, we're often convinced that doing things God's way will only limit and restrict us. We must understand that being a producer and a steward often involves sacrifices that will take us away from our natural inclinations.

When we choose not to work our blessings, something will die. God told Adam in **Genesis 2:17**, "But you must not eat from the tree of the knowledge of good and evil, for when you eat of it you will surely die." Something always dies when we don't follow God's plan. Resources and relationships are meant to be worked, both according to God's plan. Adam and Eve suffered death in both of these areas. They were kicked out of the garden and they damaged their relationship with each other and with God.

Don't work your way into misery

What a shame to have every material thing in the world that you want and still be totally miserable. King Solomon is a good example of this in Ecclesiastes 2:7-11.

[7] I bought male and female slaves and had other slaves who were born in my house. I also owned more herds and flocks than anyone in Jerusalem before me. [8] I amassed silver and gold for myself, and the treasure of kings and provinces. I acquired men and women singers, and a harem as well—the delights of the heart of man. [9] I became greater by far than anyone in Jerusalem before me. In all this my wisdom stayed with me. [10] I denied myself nothing my eyes desired; I refused my heart no pleasure. My heart took delight in all my work, and this was the reward for all my labor. [11] Yet when I surveyed all that my hands had done and what I had toiled to achieve, everything was meaningless, a chasing after the wind; nothing was gained under the sun.

Solomon worked his blessings, but at one point ended up miserable. We don't have to be millionaires for that same depressing feeling to come over us. It can surface no matter what our salary if we haven't learned to be better stewards. Solomon labored for selfish accumulation, not for the kingdom of God. Just as God guarded the entrance to the Garden of Eden, He is guarding the entrance to abundant life with a clear message. If you want it, come get it. But it's going to take a servant's heart and a steward's mind instead of a consumer's greed.

Working your blessing by giving to others

Genesis 18:7 gives an example of how Abraham worked his blessing.

[7] Then he ran to the herd and selected a choice, tender calf and gave it to a servant, who hurried to prepare it.

After the Lord appeared unto Abraham and sent him guests, Abraham went out and got a choice calf for dinner. The fact that he was able to choose from a herd shows his steward's mind and indicates that he knew how to work his blessing. Without the mindset of a producer, Abraham would not have had a herd from which to make a selection. The fact that he gave his best for others shows his servant's heart. Abraham didn't hesitate to select a tender calf to prepare for his guests. Are you giving God your best? It's hard to give God your best when you're not working your blessing, because it often feels like not enough is coming in and you want to keep the best for yourself.

Good stewardship provides you with ample to share with others. Stewardship, however, is hard work and we don't always want to work. We sometimes would rather eat and spend on ourselves and let others take care of themselves.

Working your blessing by working your talents

We would be hard pressed to find a better example of how God requires us to work our blessing than the parable of the talents found in Matthew 25:14-30:

[14]"Again, it will be like a man going on a journey, who called his servants and entrusted his property to them. [15]To one he gave five talents of money, to another two talents, and to another one talent, each according to his ability. Then he went on his journey. [16]The man who had received the five talents went at once and put his money to work and gained five more. [17]So also, the one with the two talents gained two more. [18]But the man who had received the one talent went off, dug a hole in the ground and hid his master's money. [19]"After a long time the master of those servants returned and settled accounts with them. [20]The man who had received the five talents brought the other five. 'Master,' he said, 'you entrusted me with five talents. See, I have gained five more.' [21]"His master replied, 'Well done, good and faithful servant! You have been faithful with a few things; I will put you in charge of many things. Come and share your master's happiness!' [22]"The man with the two talents also came. 'Master,' he said, 'you entrusted me with two talents; see, I have gained two more.' [23]"His master replied, 'Well done, good and faithful servant! You have been faithful with a few things; I will put you in charge of many things. Come and share your master's happiness!' [24]"Then the man who had received the one talent came. 'Master,' he said, 'I knew that you are a hard man, harvesting where you have not sown and gathering where you have not scattered seed. [25]So I was afraid and went out and hid your talent in the ground. See, here is what belongs to you.' [26]"His master replied, 'You wicked, lazy servant! So you knew that I harvest where I have not sown and gather where I have not scattered seed? [27]Well then, you should have put my money on deposit with the bankers, so that when I returned I would have received it back with interest. [28]" 'Take the talent from him and give it to the one who has the ten talents. [29]For everyone who has will be given more, and he will have an abundance. Whoever does not have, even what he has will be taken from him. [30]And throw that worthless servant outside, into the darkness, where there will be weeping and gnashing of teeth.'

The first two servants multiplied their talents, while the third servant hid his. What talents are lying dormant inside us that could be used for the kingdom? Hiding our talents is the same as wasting them because nobody is getting any benefit from them. God has not given us the spirit of fear. We must walk out in faith and work our blessings for the sake of the Kingdom.

In verse 24 the servant paints a picture of the man (God) being unfair. This is the viewpoint of someone who is selfish and doesn't want to even try. We often think God is being too hard, or unfair and is not taking into consideration our situation. We, therefore, want God to exempt us from being productive until we feel our blessing is big enough to work.

God's position has not and will not change: If He blesses us with anything, He expects us to work it to His glory. Whatever He gives us, He expects us to turn it into something more.

We have to change how we think and spend money. We can't continue to take pride in our ability to stretch or save a dollar when God has equipped us to multiply it. We're not all going to turn major profits for the kingdom, but we all are expected to attempt to do something. God is not too hard on us. He is not demanding a certain level of productivity from us, but He is reprimanding our inactivity. God is loving and merciful, but the problem He had with this servant was that he wasn't even putting forth the minimum effort.

Life Speaks

One of the best ways to use your talents is to first find something you enjoy doing. I like woodworking. I don't spend a lot of time doing it, but around the holidays and when the seasons change, I create various works and engrave them with Bible verses. I sell quite a few of these and give just as many away. It doesn't bring in much money, but I enjoy the extra pocket change and the smiles my work brings from others whom I bless. More than anything else, this activity helps to keep my entrepreneurial juices flowing.

Jacob works his blessing

In the previous unit we detailed Jacob's battle with getting to his blessings. He had his issues, like we all do, but overall Jacob was an excellent example of how to work your blessing.

> [27] But Laban said to him, "If I have found favor in your eyes, please stay. I have learned by divination that the LORD has blessed me because of you." [28] He added, "Name your wages, and I will pay them."
>
> —Genesis 30:27,28

Laban, Jacob's father-in-law, prospered tremendously because Jacob knew how to work his blessings. One day Jacob told Laban he was leaving to establish his own legacy. Laban asked Jacob not to leave and offered Jacob whatever salary he wanted. Laban mistreated Jacob terribly. He tricked him into a marriage Jacob didn't want. He cheated Jacob out of money, but Laban knew how valuable Jacob was.

> [29] Jacob said to him, "You know how I have worked for you and how your livestock has fared under my care. [30] The little you had before I came has increased greatly, and the LORD has blessed you wherever I have been. But now, when may I do something for my own household?"
>
> —Genesis 30:29,30

Laban was reminded of how little he had before Jacob came to work for him. Laban didn't seem to appreciate how much Jacob had done for him until Jacob was ready to leave and work for himself. When you're working your blessing, often you will go unnoticed and unappreciated. Don't let that discourage you from doing what you know is best. God is taking you somewhere whether other people can see it or not at the time.

Life Speaks

For some reason very few people ever volunteer to teach the 5th-7th grade Sunday school class. They say the kids are a bit too wired, but I enjoy them. I guess one reason we get along so well is I make up games for them. One Bible board game in particular that they can't seem to get enough of is called, Faith Walk. I made it out of cardboard, paint, and odds and ends I found in the basement.

I took it to the parents, the church board, and the denominational leadership, but there was no interest in providing funding for marketing. They all thought it was nice but probably wouldn't have broad appeal. After two years of trying, I finally convinced a Christian game maker to give it a shot. It's not selling like Monopoly or anything like that, but it is now being sold in quite a few Christian bookstores. I still have my day job but those quarterly royalty checks are a great supplement to my income.

In Genesis 30:31-36 Jacob had a plan of taking that which was despised or insignificant and working it to prosperity. Laban had to be laughing to himself, but Jacob understood something that we need to learn. When God blesses us with something, no matter how insignificant it may appear in the world's eyes, God can still work it. We have to have faith that He will!

³¹ "What shall I give you?" he asked. "Don't give me anything," Jacob replied. "But if you will do this one thing for me, I will go on tending your flocks and watching over them: ³² Let me go through all your flocks today and remove from them every speckled or spotted sheep, every dark-colored lamb and every spotted or speckled goat. They will be my wages. ³³ And my honesty will testify for me in the future, whenever you check on the wages you have paid me. Any goat in my possession that is not speckled or spotted, or any lamb that is not dark-colored, will be considered stolen." ³⁴ "Agreed," said Laban. "Let it be as you have said." ³⁵ That same day he removed all the male goats that were streaked or spotted, and all the speckled or spotted female goats (all that had white on them) and all the dark-colored lambs, and he placed them in the care of his sons. ³⁶ Then he put a three-day journey between himself and Jacob, while Jacob continued to tend the rest of Laban's flocks.

—Geness 30:31-36

Jacob told Laban, "You take the best, I'll take the worst. You take the many, I'll take the few." Jacob knew that the God he served would prosper him in the end. Genesis 30:37-42 reveals Jacob's plan for success. The results of Jacob's working his blessings are seen in Genesis 30:43.

[43] In this way the man grew exceedingly prosperous and came to own large flocks, and maidservants and menservants, and camels and donkeys.

Five concepts on working your blessing

In the following verses Jacob tells Laban how he worked his blessing. There are five concepts that we want to pick up from these verses.

[38] "I have been with you for twenty years now. Your sheep and goats have not miscarried, nor have I eaten rams from your flocks. [39] I did not bring you animals torn by wild beasts; I bore the loss myself. And you demanded payment from me for whatever was stolen by day or night. [40] This was my situation: The heat consumed me in the daytime and the cold at night, and sleep fled from my eyes. [41] It was like this for the twenty years I was in your household. I worked for you fourteen years for your two daughters and six years for your flocks, and you changed my wages ten times. [42] If the God of my father, the God of Abraham and the Fear of Isaac, had not been with me, you would surely have sent me away empty-handed. But God has seen my hardship and the toil of my hands, and last night he rebuked you."

—Genesis 31:38-42

Concept #1: Jacob worked for Laban twenty years. Working your blessing is a process that involves time. You must not become discouraged if God does not prosper you within the timetable that you have set.

Concept #2: "Your sheep and goats have not miscarried." To work our blessings we must spend time with and nurture them or else they will not survive. How many of us have started to pursue a goal and then aborted it? "I'm going to open my own business. I'm going to go back to school. I'm going to write a book. I'm going to…." By aborting our plans and dreams, we destroy that which God has blessed us with. We have to nurture our dreams or they will die early.

Concept #3: "Nor have I eaten the rams from your flock." Jacob made Laban rich even though Laban treated him unfairly. Jacob could have easily justified eating Laban's steaks every night. But Jacob knew that in order to prosper, he couldn't be consumption minded or vengeful.

Concept #4: "I bore the loss myself." When we work our blessings, we have to be willing to accept setbacks and be willing to make sacrifices. They may seem unfair to us, but we keep going because we have a vision of our long-range goal.

Concept #5: When we work our blessings, we understand what commitment is all about. We press on through the adverse circumstances. Fluctuations in the climate—be they physical, economical, social, political, spiritual, or whatever—don't bother us. We press on. Extra sleep is often a luxury.

These are five keys to how Jacob worked his blessing.

Joseph works his blessing

Joseph was thrown into a pit and left for dead by his brothers. He was then removed from the pit, sold into slavery, and later imprisoned. Joseph persevered through all this because he knew God had a plan for his life. He knew God favored him and was with him despite the trials he endured.

> [2] The LORD was with Joseph and he prospered, and he lived in the house of his Egyptian master. [3] When his master saw that the LORD was with him and that the LORD gave him success in everything he did, [4] Joseph found favor in his eyes and became his attendant. Potiphar put him in charge of his household, and he entrusted to his care everything he owned.
>
> —Genesis 39:2-4

Joseph learned how to maneuver through adversity. He was blessed because God was with him. That doesn't happen by accident, but by obedience. Notice that Potiphar didn't say Joseph was smart or lucky. Potiphar knew that Joseph's success came from God because Joseph talked about God. Joseph gave God the glory for everything. That's how you work your blessing. You don't try to get people to see you; people begin to see how God is working in you.

Joseph became a trusted confidant to Pharoah and God blessed and promoted him as he continued to be a blessing to his employer.

³³ "And now let Pharaoh look for a discerning and wise man and put him in charge of the land of Egypt. ³⁴ Let Pharaoh appoint commissioners over the land to take a fifth of the harvest of Egypt during the seven years of abundance. ³⁵ They should collect all the food of these good years that are coming and store up the grain under the authority of Pharaoh, to be kept in the cities for food. ³⁶ This food should be held in reserve for the country, to be used during the seven years of famine that will come upon Egypt, so that the country may not be ruined by the famine."

—Genesis 41:33-36

Joseph was able to work his blessing because he had an open line of communication with God. God said that there would be seven good years, and then seven bad years would follow. Joseph told Pharaoh to find someone who could manage the crops during the good times so there would be provision during the famine.

³⁷ The plan seemed good to Pharaoh and to all his officials. ³⁸ So Pharaoh asked them, "Can we find anyone like this man, one in whom is the spirit of God?" ³⁹ Then Pharaoh said to Joseph, "Since God has made all this known to you, there is no one so discerning and wise as you. ⁴⁰ You shall be in charge of my palace, and all my people are to submit to your orders. Only with respect to the throne will I be greater than you."

—Genesis 41:37-40

Joseph didn't have to volunteer for the job. Pharaoh had seen the wisdom of Joseph. He had witnessed God working through Joseph and therefore knew Joseph was the best man for the job. People may not always share your faith, but when they realize that you have special talent, they learn to depend on you.

⁵⁴ and the seven years of famine began, just as Joseph had said. There was famine in all the other lands, but in the whole land of Egypt there was food.

—Genesis 41:54

The famine came and impacted everybody except those who were with Joseph in Egypt. Joseph had wisely stored grain during the good years. If we are content to be the ultimate consumer and are always preoccupied with the good times, we will often never see what hit us until it's too late. When we work our blessings we become a benefit to others as well as ourselves, especially during hard times.

[56] When the famine had spread over the whole country, Joseph opened the storehouses and sold grain to the Egyptians, for the famine was severe throughout Egypt. [57] And all the countries came to Egypt to buy grain from Joseph, because the famine was severe in all the world.

—Genesis 41:56,57

Working your blessings creates opportunities for you. People begin to come to you. Your services can become priceless and this positions you to further work your blessing.

Life Speaks

It's not like I'm running a business, but it's amazing how everybody who comes up with an idea wants to talk to me. It's a good feeling to have people value my opinion. I'm not sure who gets encouraged the most by our conversations, me or them! One of the main things I tell people is that it doesn't always have to be the other guy. God has blessed all of us with different gifts and abilities that, when cultivated, bring Him glory and motivate us to get more out of life.

Working our blessings means breaking the cycle of consumerism and learning to become better stewards of God's provisions. When we get serious about our stewardship we'll see more of the abundant life, not only for ourselves, but for others as well. We must follow the examples outlined in Scripture. For as Romans 15:4 states, **"For everything that was written in the past was written to teach us, so that through endurance and the encouragement of the Scriptures we might have hope."**

We must learn how to work our blessings, to endure, and encourage ourselves in the Scriptures when things are not looking up. We need to gain hope from the testimonies of great people of faith in the Bible who knew how to work their blessings.

There was no maintenance with manna. It was fresh and new every morning. It would be nice if we had a totally new start every day, but that's not the reality we live in. For while God's mercies are new every morning to encourage and strengthen us, we don't awake to new manna. We still awake to face old issues—issues that have to be worked if we are to be blessed.

Unit Review

1. T/F ____ Working your blessing is all about being a more informed consumer.

   T/F ____ Being a producer involves sacrifices that often go against our natural inclinations.

   T/F ____ When we fail to work our blessings, something usually dies.

2. To work our blessings in a way that won't cause misery, we have to have a servant's _____ and a steward's _____ instead of a consumer's _____.

3. Why will God not exempt us from working our talents no matter how insignificant we think they are?

   _____

   _____

   _____

   _____

   _____

   _____

4. What stands out most to you on how Jacob worked his blessing?

   _____

   _____

   _____

   _____

   _____

   _____

5. From the example of Joseph we can see that working our blessings can create
   _____ for us.

6. What are the five concepts on working your blessing that were presented in this
   unit?

   _____

   _____

   _____

   _____

   _____

7. Bryan seemed to be very enterprising, yet he was patient. He was the type of
   person who received just as much enjoyment from the journey as he did arriv-
   ing at his destination. Explain how important this is when you are working your
   blessing.

   _____

   _____

   _____

   _____

   _____

8. What, if any, revelation has God spoken to you from this unit?

   _____

   _____

   _____

   _____

   _____

9. What action items can you develop to apply the concepts of this unit?

Action Item #1:

_____

_____

_____

Action Item #2:

_____

_____

_____

Unit Jewel:

We can't continue to take pride in our ability to stretch or save a dollar when God has equipped us to multiply it.

Unit Summary:

To work our blessings for maximum benefit, we must not just be consumer minded. We have to begin to think and act like producers.

Meditation/Prayer Focus:

Commit to the Lord whatever you do, and your plans will succeed.

—Proverbs 16:3

Lord, You have already blessed me. Now I must work my blessings for Your glory.

The Spiritual Side of Riches

Life Speaks: Danielle Swanson

My colleagues don't understand me. They ask, "Danielle, why would a successful, single neurosurgeon live as modestly as you do?" I live in a 20-year-old four-bedroom ranch with my beagle, Rusty. I buy my cars used, and I seldom travel or spend on clothes. The point that people miss is that I am happy and fulfilled! Through my career, and the salary it provides, I have the opportunity to make such an impact on the lives of so many people.

If my friends must know, I give 12% of my income to my church. 10% more goes to foreign mission work. Another 10% goes to various local, national, and international food and medical relief efforts. I don't have to publicize what I do because I am totally content being the woman God has called me to be. My colleagues want me to act rich. The more I think about it—I already am!

Getting rich vs being rich.

Everybody wants to get rich, but do we really know how to be rich? Being rich is more than simply spending money and being happy, for the happiness found in being financially rich can be wonderful, yet short-lived. Quite often the wealthy run out of happiness well before they run out of money. Of course we should be rich in love, friends, and peace, but how about financially? There is no shortage of people giving instruction on how to get rich, but very few teaching us how to be rich.

Rich toward God

What does God require of us when we become rich? God requires us to be rich toward Him. In Matthew chapter 19 Jesus talked about the difficulty of a rich man getting into heaven. In Matthew chapter 13 Jesus spoke of the deceitfulness of riches. In Luke chapter 16 Jesus gave the parable of the rich man in hell. Often these verses are interpreted as Jesus being against riches. In Luke 12:16-21 Jesus gives us a parable that brings the needed balance.

> [16]And he told them this parable: "The ground of a certain rich man produced a good crop. [17]He thought to himself, 'What shall I do? I have no place to store my crops.' [18]"Then he said, 'This is what I'll do. I will tear down my barns and build bigger ones, and there I will store all my grain and my goods. [19]And I'll say to myself, "You have plenty of good things laid up for many years. Take life easy; eat, drink and be merry." ' [20]"But God said to him, 'You fool! This very night your life will be demanded from you. Then who will get what you have prepared for yourself?' [21]"This is how it will be with anyone who stores up things for himself but is not rich toward God."

God didn't have a problem with this man or anybody else having wealth. The problem is when our riches are not toward God. In other words, this man only knew the natural side of riches. He only knew how to use his resources to benefit himself and not the kingdom of God.

Money, whether you have too little or too much, is a magnet for problems. This is why David wrote in **Proverbs 30:8**, "Give me neither poverty nor riches." David wanted to be somewhere comfortably in the middle. We can all agree that poverty has its problems, but if we don't understand the spiritual side of riches, an abundance of money can cause its share of misery as well.

The spiritual purpose of riches

In Deuteronomy chapter 8, God reminded the Israelites to continually keep His commandments and never forget the God who delivered them and His purpose for blessing them.

> [18]But you shall [earnestly] remember the Lord your God, for it is He Who gives you power to get wealth, that He may establish His covenant which He swore to your fathers, as it is this day.
>
> —Deuteronomy 8:18 (AMP)

God empowers us to get wealth for the purpose of promoting His kingdom. That's His primary reason for blessing us with more than we need. It doesn't mean we can't improve our lifestyles, but would we ever consider using that same amount of money, above tithes and offerings, to advance the kingdom of God?

Life Speaks

Okay! I'll admit, growing up in New York I've come to love Broadway productions and sports. Whether it's "Phantom of the Opera" or "Cats," the Knicks, Giants, or Yankees, it doesn't matter; I enjoy going out—it's how I unwind. The tickets and seats I get aren't cheap either, but I don't feel guilty spending the money because what I give to the kingdom is so much more. I'm convinced that God has blessed me with the resources I have to meet my basic needs, to further His kingdom, and to enjoy life as I see fit. Keeping that order goes to the core of who I am.

Abundance vs prioritized giving

[41]Jesus sat down opposite the place where the offerings were put and watched the crowd putting their money into the temple treasury. Many rich people threw in large amounts. [42]But a poor widow came and put in two very small copper coins, worth only a fraction of a penny. [43]Calling his disciples to him, Jesus said, "I tell you the truth, this poor widow has put more into the treasury than all the others. [44]They all gave out of their wealth; but she, out of her poverty, put in everything—all she had to live on."

—Mark 12:41-44

Being rich toward God is more than giving out of our abundance. It's no great accomplishment and takes very little faith to tithe when you have millions. When God begins to flow more money to us, He is very interested in how much we recycle back into the kingdom.

When we understand the spiritual side of riches, we view the tithe, not as a destination point or a cut off point, but as a starting point. If we view tithing as a final goal, then we are not even close to being prepared for the riches we would like God to send our way. It doesn't excite God when we give out of excess whether it's five or five million dollars. He expects our giving to the kingdom to be prioritized not in place of, but above our personal desires.

God can cover those bad investments

When we don't understand the spiritual side of riches, we will make bad financial investments. We will make deals with the wrong people. We do these things to gain something that we are not trusting God to give us.

Amaziah was king of Jerusalem. In preparation for a particular battle he hired 100,000 soldiers who were not approved of by God.

> [7] But a man of God came to him and said, "O king, these troops from Israel must not march with you, for the LORD is not with Israel—not with any of the people of Ephraim. [8] Even if you go and fight courageously in battle, God will overthrow you before the enemy, for God has the power to help or to overthrow." [9] Amaziah asked the man of God, "But what about the hundred talents I paid for these Israelite troops?" The man of God replied, "The LORD can give you much more than that."
>
> —2 Chronicles 25:7-9

Amaziah didn't feel that he could trust God for his victory so he hired an army to help him fight his battle. The man of God came and told Amaziah that he was paying man for an outcome that only God controlled. Amaziah knew the right thing to do, but his mind was on the money he had already invested. What do you do about the money you already have tied up in a bad investment? The man of God left it open by saying God is able to give you much more than this.

Understanding the spiritual side of riches is realizing that God can more than cover your bad investments. Will you believe this and turn them over to God, or will you continue with a plan that is destined to fail? By knowing what God is able to do, you don't have to be so set on continuing your investment or recovering your losses. Remember, you're looking for God to bless you in a way far greater than the amount of your ill-advised investment. That has to become your new focus.

Whose debts are you covering?

The book of Philemon tells the story of Onesimus, a runaway slave who became a Christian. Onesimus was doing well spiritually and showed great promise for service. Paul recognized the potential in Onesimus and wrote a letter to Philemon, his owner, to cover the debt of Onesimus. In that letter Paul wrote:

> [18]If he has done you any wrong or owes you anything, charge it to me.
>
> —Philemon 1:18

Grasping the spiritual side of riches means understanding that just as God covers our bad debts and investments, we need to do the same for others in the body of Christ. This doesn't mean that once we become rich we pay off everybody's credit card bills in the church. What it means is as we encounter people who are making positive changes in their lives and doing their best to serve God at a higher level, we prayerfully consider teaming with them to share their financial burdens. It means we assist God in helping them to spiritually become what God is calling them to be. We become spiritual entrepreneurs looking for talent to invest in. We do this realizing that as the people we invest in continue to grow spiritually, they'll be an even greater asset to the kingdom.

Blessing those who carry the gospel

Paul explains the benefit of understanding the spiritual side of riches and teaming with someone who is doing a great work for the Lord. Paul was in jail for preaching the gospel and had no way of creating income for himself, yet his heart's desire was to continue to spread the gospel.

[15]Moreover, as you Philippians know, in the early days of your acquaintance with the gospel, when I set out from Macedonia, not one church shared with me in the matter of giving and receiving, except you only; [16]for even when I was in Thessalonica, you sent me aid again and again when I was in need. [17]Not that I am looking for a gift, but I am looking for what may be credited to your account.

—Philippians 4:15-17

The church at Philippi was the only church that was sending Paul money so the ministry could continue. Paul made it plain that he wasn't looking for any money, but explained that when the Philippians gave to the ministry, God made a credit into their spiritual bank account. Understanding the spiritual side of riches is realizing that you are blessing yourself by being a financial blessing to those who are on the front line spreading the gospel.

Life Speaks

My pastor is the most humble and dedicated man of God I know. I really don't think the church realizes how blessed we are to have him, and unfortunately it shows in the salary he is paid. His sermons and guidance have been life-changing for me, and the last thing I want him worrying about is financial concerns. Each month I send him an anonymous encouragement card with Galatians 6:6 written in it, "Anyone who receives instruction in the word must share all good things with his instructor." Inside the card I always include a generous cash gift to show my appreciation for the many sacrifices he makes.

Joseph of Arimathaea

After Jesus was crucified, Joseph of Arimathaea requested the body of Jesus from the authorities. We can learn numerous lessons on the spiritual side of riches by examining how Joseph went about doing this.

[57]As evening approached, there came a rich man from Arimathea, named Joseph, who had himself become a disciple of Jesus. [58]Going to Pilate, he asked for Jesus' body, and Pilate ordered that it be given to him. [59]Joseph took the body, wrapped it in a clean linen

cloth, [60]and placed it in his own new tomb that he had cut out of the rock. He rolled a big stone in front of the entrance to the tomb and went away.

—Matthew 27:57-60

This is an example of someone who was not only rich but also a disciple of Jesus. Joseph understood the spiritual side of riches. The text mentions that he was rich and also a disciple of Jesus, but that didn't necessarily have to be the order that he prioritized things. Sometimes people may see your house or your car and think that you're rich before they get a chance to know that you're a Christian. That's OK. By your conversation and actions people will quickly be able to tell what your priorities are.

Let's look at the actions of Joseph. First he went to Pilate. The very act of someone associated with Jesus going to Pilate was a dangerous move. He could have lost his life, his money, or both. Understanding the spiritual side of riches causes us to realize that the spiritual must be placed before riches at all cost. Joseph could have easily paid someone else to go and take the risk, but he went himself.

Next, Joseph asked for the body of Jesus. Joseph was rich, but he was a humble man. He could have gone to Pilate and brashly tried to throw his financial weight around. Understanding the spiritual side of riches is knowing that money is not the resolution to every situation. Many rich people tend to address every situation with their money. Joseph addressed the situation with his heart.

Joseph then wrapped the body of Jesus in clean linen. The spiritual side of riches is understanding that you've been blessed to give Jesus your best. Notice it doesn't say that this rich man hired two people to carry the body of Jesus. Maybe he did, but he obviously was personally involved as well. Acknowledging the spiritual side of riches brings the understanding that we are servants of the most high God. Despite our financial status, there is no job that is beneath us in the service of our Lord and Savior, Jesus Christ.

Joseph took the body of Jesus and put it in his own tomb. This was a specially-cut tomb made just for Joseph. They didn't have power tools back then. Who knows how long it would have taken for someone to make Joseph another tomb. Suppose Joseph died? Where would he be buried? I don't think that even mattered to Joseph at the time.

When you are living on the spiritual side of riches, critical kingdom needs of today often outweigh our potential needs of tomorrow. We have been blessed to offer our best for the kingdom of God when it is most needed, not when it's most convenient.

Understanding these key points to the spiritual side of riches is not something we can do after we become rich. We must begin to train ourselves in this mindset now, or our chances of becoming rich at the hand of God are greatly decreased.

What does this have to do with me?

In the following verse Paul was sharing with the Corinthian church some of the hardships that he endured. He was encouraging them to understand that no matter what you're going through and how little you think you have, when you are spiritually rich and understand the spiritual side of riches you still have much to give.

> [10]As grieved and mourning, yet [we are] always rejoicing; as poor [ourselves, yet] bestowing riches on many; as having nothing, and [yet in reality] possessing all things.
> —2 Corinthians 6:10 (AMP)

When you live a life dependent on manna, you feel there is no reason to rejoice. It seems impossible to be rich toward God or others, because in your eyes there are no riches! With manna there is just enough for today; nothing to save, invest, or share. It is therefore impossible to experience the spiritual side of riches until our lives are manna-free.

God wants to know if we're going to pout about our current financial situation or if we're going to joyfully use what we have for His glory. God is testing us to find out if we can handle being greatly blessed financially. He wants to see if we have the courage to follow biblical principles by faith while we have what seems like nothing. Because no matter how little or how much we have, we have been blessed to be a blessing to someone else. This is the key to understanding the spiritual side of riches.

Unit Review

1. What does it mean to be rich toward God?

   _____

   _____

   _____

   _____

2. How do we balance the spiritual purpose for riches mentioned in Deuteronomy 8:18 with our desires for material things above what we need?

   _____

   _____

   _____

   _____

3. Check the correct answer.

   ____ The tithe should be a destination point in our giving.

   ____ The tithe should be a starting point in our giving.

   ____ The tithe should be a cut-off point in our giving.

4. T/F ____ As long as we give tithes and offerings, God is not concerned with what we do with the rest of our money.

   T/F ____ When God allows money to flow to us, He is concerned with how we recycle it into the kingdom.

   T/F ____ God expects our giving to be prioritized not in place of, but above our personal desires.

5. What two concepts on covering debt were covered in this unit?

_____

_____

_____

_____

_____

6. Being rich doesn't mean you always approach every situation with your money in order to get what you want. How was Joseph of Arimathaea a good example of this?

_____

_____

_____

_____

_____

7. You have been blessed to offer your best for the kingdom of God when it is most _____, not when it's most _____.

8. Danielle said she was giving a third of her income to the work of the kingdom. Do you think she mentioned all of her giving? Some people just have good hearts, but what would it take for average persons to develop the frame of mind to donate such a large percentage of their income to God's work?

_____

_____

_____

_____

9. What, if any, revelation has God spoken to you from this unit?

    _____

    _____

    _____

10. What action items can you develop to apply the concepts of this unit?

    Action Item #1:

    _____

    _____

    Action Item #2:

    _____

    _____

Unit Jewel:

When we understand the spiritual side of riches, we view the tithe not as a destination point, or a cut-off point, but as a starting point.

Unit Summary:

There is a spiritual side of riches that calls us to be rich toward God. Understanding this requires us to view our resources as assets for building the kingdom.

Meditation/Prayer Focus:

Remember this: Whosoever sows sparingly will also reap sparingly, and whosoever sows generously will also reap generously.

—2 Corinthians 9:6

Lord, expand my vision that I might clearly see the needs of the kingdom. Then, as I use what I have, increase my resources to help me meet even greater needs.

Thoroughly Furnished

Life Speaks: Jason Phelps

I remember my run-down two-bedroom apartment, my eleven-year-old Buick, and a job that paid $200 a month less than what I needed to pay my bills. Now I have a 4,500 square foot home sitting on five wooded acres overlooking a lake, a detached six-car garage and shop to pursue my passion for automobiles new and old, and a thriving business that allows me to work when I want to and travel when I don't. This was a dream come true, but it wasn't my goal.

I grew up in a home where church attendance was part of the weekly routine. I learned enough in church to feel guilty about my teenage actions, but not guilty enough to change. Yet, through all the drugs, sex, alcohol, and misconduct, God preserved me and allowed me to have my fill. I was eternally grateful for His hand of mercy and vowed as a young adult to seek fulfillment in Him as passionately as I sought my much regrettable fulfillment in the world. I allowed Jesus to drastically change my life and was pleasantly surprised when He allowed me to just as dramatically change my lifestyle.

The thoroughly-furnished life

The phrase "thoroughly furnished" might bring to mind an elaborately decorated home. Thoroughly furnished also means fully equipped, which might cause you to think of a luxury car with every imaginable upgrade. Thoroughly furnished means you are loaded, you have the total package. When we neglect our Source (God) and abuse our resources (money), we let the world talk us into having expensive taste that doesn't match our income. We then go after a thoroughly-furnished lifestyle and end up in Struggle Class.

Let's put the dream house and dream car on hold for a minute. Let's take our minds off the Hollywood lifestyle with all of its glitter and flare, and focus on the thoroughly-furnished life. When Matthew 6:33 says, **"But seek first his kingdom and his righteousness, and all these things will be given to you as well,"** how do you think those things will be given to you? Again, God is not going to miraculously drop blessings out of the sky. The manna has ceased.

Our giving, however, causes others to begin giving to us. When we truly live for God, we are then best positioned to receive increase through the hand of man. People become aware of just how valuable we are and our services become in high demand for what we can bring into their lives.

We saw this in previous units with Laban seeking to retain Jacob's services and Potiphar promoting Joseph. Another example is in Daniel 2:48 where King Nebuchadnezar realized the resourcefulness of Daniel, made him a great ruler, and gave him gifts.

When we seek God and allow Him to mold and shape us, He blesses us with wisdom that manifests itself in various areas of our lives. If we lack this wisdom, as well as an above-average work ethic, all we will get is a taste of what many call the good life. All we can talk about is the Rolls Royce that we touched or the mansion we visited once. All we get is a taste. Expensive taste without the wisdom of God is a ticket to Struggle Class.

Life Speaks

I had no idea how my life would be changed by answering the ad in the newspaper. The position was for a manufacturing assistant in a small plastics factory. All I knew was that I had blown a lot of good jobs in the past and it was time for me to finally take something seriously. With my past sinful life behind me, I had been seeking God fervently and prayed asking Him to provide me with a good job. Mark Ligenfelter, the owner, hired me and was immediately impressed with my passion to learn and my work ethic. Mark regularly increased my responsibilities and pay.

After five years I became plant manager and was constantly questioning Mark about all aspects of the business. Long story short, Mark treated me like the son he never had. I had made arrangements to buy the business from Mark when he retired in eight years. Mark suddenly became ill, however, and on his deathbed willed the business over to me. All I did differently was bring in a fresh marketing approach that increased the company's exposure, and business has been growing exponentially every since. I didn't deserve this opportunity, but I'm sure that God was pleased with how quickly I made a 180 degree turn in my life to live for Him.

Haste doesn't always make waste

In the following verses, David said he thought about how he was walking and then turned his feet to God's ways. David realized that he had wasted a lot of time doing things his way and against God's wishes. To make sure he didn't waste any more time, he quickly brought himself in alignment with the Word of God.

[59] I have considered my ways and have turned my steps to your statutes. [60] I will hasten and not delay to obey your commands.

—Psalms 119:59,60

The tools we need to have a successful life with all the trappings are found in the Bible. Our problem is impatience. Because of our haste, we see a lot of waste: wasted years, energy, and money. Because of our haste we only get a taste. We can't be hasty about the next business deal or decision that can potentially bring us more material possessions. Instead, we must be like David. We must redeem the time and make haste to line ourselves up with God's Word.

What's the profit margin?

If our goal is to obtain a thoroughly-furnished lifestyle, then there has to be financial profit generated from somewhere. The following verses, however, speak of the spiritual profit that we need to see so that our lives are first put in order.

> [16]All Scripture is given by inspiration of God, and is profitable for doctrine, for reproof, for correction, for instruction in righteousness: [17]that the man of God may be perfect, thoroughly furnished unto all good works.
>
> —In 2 Timothy 3:16,17 (KJV)

While we may have visions of a glamorous lifestyle, God wants our lives to be thoroughly equipped. God wants to freely give us the tools to be successful in life. The holdup is we don't always believe that God's tools are profitable. The delay is that we look for financial profitability to the neglect of spiritual profitability. When you believe something will turn a profit for you, then you don't mind investing in it. If you're not going to church, reading your Bible, tithing, fasting, praying, serving, then you must not believe that investing in those things will return a profit—spiritual or financial.

The Bible is profitable for doctrine, reproof, correction, and instruction. You might say, "That's fine, but where is money in that list?" That's the whole point! Third John 2 (AMP) says, **"Beloved, I pray that you may prosper in every way and [that your body] may keep well, even as [I know] your soul keeps well and prospers."** God doesn't want us to have a thoroughly-furnished lifestyle if we don't have a thoroughly-furnished life. This is why Adam and Eve were driven from the Garden of Eden. Through life choices they forfeited their right to God's best.

If we want to make an investment and see immediate financial profit, even from the world's point of view that's not an investment; that's either gambling or illegal. If our desire to know God doesn't match our expensive taste, we will gamble and do things like the world does in an attempt to achieve all we want from life.

In order to obtain a life of abundance, we have to accept the fact that the profitability we seek is first indirect before it's direct. It's first spiritual before it's financial. God wants us to spiritually develop our lives so we can handle whatever lifestyle comes our way.

We have to get to the point where we value spiritual profitability more than we do financial. We have to delay our financially-expensive taste and start making some spiritually-expensive decisions.

Decision #1: The first decision we have to make is to accept the fact that the Scriptures are inspired of God. That's expensive because if the Bible is not just a bunch of manmade words, then we have to trade in our personal doctrine for what the Bible says. We may have to reevaluate some things we do and relationships we have. That can be very expensive emotionally, socially, and in other ways, and we will only do it if we believe there's a profit in it for us.

Decision #2: We have to make the decision to let the Word of God reprove us. Reproof means to tell a fault. It is very costly to our pride to let the Word of God expose our faults. We won't allow this to happen unless we believe it's profitable.

Decision #3: We have to make the decision to open ourselves up to correction, realizing that God has placed spiritually-mature people in our lives to help keep us on track. This is also expensive to our pride, and again we won't buy into it unless we feel we will see a profit.

Decision #4: We have to make the decision that we need instruction from the Word of God. Going to classes, reading books, listening to tapes, and going to seminars to gain instruction is very expensive time and moneywise. Making these types of investments is very unlikely unless we believe they will be profitable.

When we begin to see the value and "spiritual" profit margin associated with doing these things, then our lives will become thoroughly furnished and our good works will become profitable to others. As Proverbs 18:16 says, your gift will make room for you. Blessings will come your way that will enable you to pursue a thoroughly-furnished lifestyle, if you so desire.

Life Speaks

I want to be more than a Christian whose only testimony is how God made me rich. I want my testimony to be about what I'm currently doing for God in appreciation for what He's done for me. I'm just as busy as the next guy, if not more, but my commitment to the kingdom costs me more in time and energy because I've been blessed with more.

"To whom much is given much is required," (Luke 12:48) and I have been given a lot. It really doesn't require a lot of me to write out a weekly four-digit tithe check. I have to show God more than a committed checkbook; I have to show Him a committed life! Whether it's Sunday morning service, Sunday school, Bible study, small group, community service, or witnessing—I'm there for it all; leading, following, participating.

When people who know me look at my luxury cars or expensive suits, hopefully they don't see status symbols. I hope they see a quality individual who happens to be inside a quality item. I truly believe that God keeps blessing me because He sees my determination and the lengths I go to in obedience and service to let my light outshine my money.

Protecting your investment

The value of having a thoroughly-furnished life is that you see how you are profiting and you want to protect your investment. Sin becomes too expensive for you. When you look at all your blessings and how God is using you, you tell yourself, "I can't afford to sin." So now you have a double incentive not to sin. Not only is it wrong, but it is a threat to all you have accomplished and obtained.

We know that sin is evil, but when our lives are not fully equipped, we ask ourselves, "What have I got to lose? I know I shouldn't be sinning, but my life hasn't turned out the way I wanted it to, so what have I got to lose?" You may not think you have much, but when the little that you do have is gone, you miss it terribly. The problem with not having a thoroughly-furnished life is that it causes us to make decisions that make our lives worse and moves us even farther from the lifestyle we desire.

When our lives are fully equipped spiritually they are fruitful, and the more fruit we're producing the less likely we are to take a bite out of a bad apple no matter how good it looks.

I can't afford to think like this!

In Matthew 5:27-30 Jesus emphasizes the role that our thought lives play in our spiritual development.

[27]"You have heard that it was said, 'Do not commit adultery.' [28]But I tell you that anyone who looks at a woman lustfully has already committed adultery with her in his heart. [29]If your right eye causes you to sin, gouge it out and throw it away. It is better for you to lose one part of your body than for your whole body to be thrown into hell. [30]And if your right hand causes you to sin, cut it off and throw it away. It is better for you to lose one part of your body than for your whole body to go into hell.

Having a thoroughly-furnished life is acknowledging that sin is not just what you do, but also what you think about doing. You realize that if your thoughts are inappropriate, they can impact your actions. Focusing on things that are contrary to God's will brings consequences that may force you to settle for far less in life than you had planned. Verses 29 and 30 stress the importance of making expensive decisions by cutting off that which can detract from the quality of life you seek to enjoy.

Offended by God?

[1]After Jesus had finished instructing his twelve disciples, he went on from there to teach and preach in the towns of Galilee. [2]When John heard in prison what Christ was doing, he sent his disciples [3]to ask him, "Are you the one who was to come, or should we expect someone else?" [4]Jesus replied, "Go back and report to John what you hear and see: [5]The blind receive sight, the lame walk, those who have leprosy are cured, the deaf hear, the dead are raised, and the good news is preached to the poor. [6]Blessed is the man who does not fall away on account of me."

—Matthew 11:1-6

To reach our life and lifestyle goals, we have to learn to be offended by the right things. We are blessed when we are not offended by God. It was as if Jesus was sending the message to John, "Do you have a problem with the good that I am doing just because you are in jail? Does it offend you?" Our problem is we tend to be offended by God when He is blessing other situations and ours is still the same.

We also have to learn to be offended by the things that give us short-term pleasure but long-term heartache. We're often offended when God says no to overeating, over spending, sex outside of marriage, inappropriate relationships, music, movies, and so forth. We begin to take sides with the temptation and ask God, "What's so wrong with this?" We are blessed when we are not offended by God who is seeking to insure that our lives are adequately prepared today for the blessings He has for us tomorrow.

Offended by God's Word?

[20]The one who received the seed that fell on rocky places is the man who hears the word and at once receives it with joy. [21]But since he has no root, he lasts only a short time. When trouble or persecution comes because of the word, he quickly falls away.

—Matthew 13:20,21

To be thoroughly furnished, we have to get rid of the stony places in our lives that keep God's Word from taking root. Without roots we cannot produce fruit, and without fruit we are not profitable. Notice that tribulation comes because of the Word. Once again, there will be things we want to do or things others want us to do that are not right based on God's Word. Will we be offended because of God's Word, or will we take the tribulation that comes when we stand faithfully on the Word of God? Even though we go to church and hear the sermon, it becomes offensive to us when we want to do what pleases us.

Stony places keep us from being properly equipped in life, which can in turn keep us from obtaining and enjoying the blessing we so desire.

The thoroughly-furnished life and lifestyle.

In the parable of the Prodigal Son, the younger son decided he didn't need the source, his father. He believed if he had the resources that he would be fine. So he left home with the intention of having the life he always dreamed of. Instead, he found himself in Struggle Class. One thing we usually miss in this parable is that both sons received their inheritance at the same time. Luke 15:12 says the father divided unto "them" his living. The older son had a choice just like the younger did. But he decided that even though he had the resources, it's best to stick with the source. This is symbolic of us always staying with God no matter how blessed we are with resources. In Luke 15:31 the father tells the oldest son, "Everything I have is yours."

There is nothing thorough about manna. Manna represents just enough to get by. Manna personifies the generic! Living on manna, therefore, is residing at the opposite end of the spectrum from a life and lifestyle that are thoroughly furnished.

When we stay faithful to the Source and do the right things with our resources, we will stay out of Struggle Class. We will develop a thoroughly-furnished life, which is the proper foundation for obtaining a thoroughly-furnished lifestyle.

Unit Review

1. What can happen when a lifestyle is thoroughly furnished, but the life is not?

    _____

    _____

    _____

    _____

2. Explain how haste can be a good thing in obtaining a thoroughly-furnished life/ lifestyle.

    _____

    _____

    _____

    _____

3. In order to have a thoroughly-furnished life we have to understand that the profitability that we seek is first s_____ before it is f_____ .

4. T/F ____ Sin becomes too expensive when you have a thoroughly-furnished life.
    T/F ____ To obtain the thoroughly-furnished life, you have to make spiritually-expensive decisions.

5. What role do offenses play in obtaining a thoroughly-furnished life and lifestyle?

    _____

    _____

    _____

    _____

6. It's easy to look at people who are wealthy, envy what they have, and question how hard they work. What do you think it would be like to be around someone like Jason?

_____

_____

_____

_____

7. What, if any, revelation has God spoken to you from this unit?

_____

_____

_____

_____

8. What action items can you develop to apply the concepts of this unit?

Action Item #1:

_____

_____

_____

_____

Action Item #2:

_____

_____

_____

_____

Unit Jewel:

When you are truly living for God and leading a thoroughly-furnished life, you are best positioned to receive what it takes to have a thoroughly-furnished lifestyle.

Unit Summary:

Our focus cannot be so much on a thoroughly-furnished lifestyle that we forget to thoroughly furnish our lives. The value of a life far outweighs the value of a lifestyle.

Meditation/Prayer Focus:

Praise the Lord. Blessed is the man who fears the Lord, who finds great delight in his commands. Wealth and riches are in his house.

—Psalms 112:1,3

Lord, let my life be as rich as I would one day like my lifestyle to be.

A Final Word

I pray that this study has provided you with a balanced and biblical guide for strengthening your relationship with God through the resources that He has placed in your stewardship. There are no shortcuts or formulas to follow, only faith and dedication to pursue the principles that have been presented. The manna has ceased, but as you stay true to His Word, the miraculous provision of God through you is just beginning. It's time to eat the fruit of Canaan. It's time for manna-free living!

Carnell Jones is the pastor of New Hope Fellowship in Bloomington, Illinois where he has served for thirteen years. He is employed as a systems analyst for a large Midwestern insurance company. He is also the creator of the best-selling Christian card game, "Amen," and a second Christian card game, "Kingdom." He is a 1983 graduate of North Carolina Central University(BBA).

Jones lives in Normal, Illinois with his wife DeLaine and their three children—Christian, Alicia, and Grant.

To order additional copies of

Manna-Free Living

Have your credit card ready and call:

1-877-421-READ (7323)

or please visit our web site at
www.pleasantword.com

Also available at:
www.amazon.com
and
www.barnesandnoble.com

Printed in the United States
34394LVS00004B/121-198